Using **SENSE** to make
DOLLAR$

Using **SENSE** to make
DOLLAR$

Godly Principles That Lead to Financial Freedom

Isaiah S. Williams, Jr., DD
with Dr. Gloria Williams

Using Sense to Make Dollars
By Isaiah S. Williams Jr., DD, with Dr. Gloria Williams
Published by Creation House
A Charisma Media Company
600 Rinehart Road
Lake Mary, Florida 32746
www.charismamedia.com

Design Director: Bill Johnson
Cover design by Terry Clifton

Visit the author's website: www.jesuspeoplemiami.org

Library of Congress Cataloging-in-Publication Data:
2013937683
International Standard Book Number: 978-1-62136-378-1
E-book International Standard Book Number:
978-1-62136-379-8

While the author has made every effort to provide accurate telephone numbers and Internet addresses at the time of publication, neither the publisher nor the author assumes any responsibility for errors or for changes that occur after publication.

First edition

13 14 15 16 17 — 9 8 7 6 5 4 3 2 1
Printed in the United States of America

DEDICATION

||||||||||||||||||||||||||||||||||||

This work is dedicated to Jesus'
people who are all over the world.
May the sound mind of Christ be
ever so abundant in the lives of
those who make up God's family.

This book is also dedicated to family
legacy. May it bring financial wisdom
to you for generations to come.

ACKNOWLEDGMENTS

||||||||||||||||||||||||||||||||||||

ACKNOWLEDGMENT AND THANKS to Alicia Wanza for her input, organization, and role in helping to make this book project happen. Thank you for your creative efforts in transcribing and editing this manuscript into book format.

Also, thanks to Joann John and Tracy Jackson for reviewing and proofing the finished manuscript.

Additionally, special thanks to Pastor Derrick Gay for his publishing knowledge and insights.

Thanks to everyone for a great team effort!

TABLE OF CONTENTS

||||||||||||||||||||||||||||||||||

INTRODUCTION

||||||||||||||||||||||||||||||||||||||

T O BE FINANCIALLY free is a wonderful state to be
in. We all look forward to a life filled with success and a bright future. We also know that we need to
experience financial freedom as a part of being able to
live the *successful, godly* life. To experience this kind of
financial freedom, we need to understand godly principles and have God-given wisdom. Understanding the
basics of these principles will lead you to:

§ *Financial increase*

§ *Financial success*

§ *Financial independence*

§ *Financial freedom*

I cannot cover every area of finance and all its
immensity in this book, but I will touch on some aspect
or part of each of the above areas.

This book will inspire you to *want* your financial freedom and the abundant life that God has promised those who follow His principles. In the following chapters, you will be challenged to get out of a life of financial debt—a life of spending money that you don't have, making decisions that prefabricate who you really are, and continuing to stay in bondage and prison to this debt with no definite release date known. Learn how to get out of fear about your future financial comfort and experience financial freedom. You'll gain the freedom to spend money that will create harmony in your life as you live knowing and representing your true financial status, which will give you freedom from an unbalanced financial scale, and peace in your financial domain.

I hope that after reading this book, you will experience increase in many areas of your life and not solely financially. As you follow the principles of God, you will gain wisdom and understanding in God's way of handling and managing your finances. As you are receptive to what you read and study in this book, it is my desire and prayer that you will produce a harvest of financial increase, financial success, financial independence, and *ultimately financial freedom.*

Chapter One

TWENTY STEPS TO A LIFE OF FINANCIAL FREEDOM

||||||||||||||||||||||||||||||||||||

A S WITH ALL things in life, there are steps of progression that we must take. Whether it be planning a family, deciding what city we want to live in, buying a new home, or choosing a career, we have to take one step at a time in the process. Therefore, it is the same when dealing with our finances and wanting to be successful in that area of our lives. Building a solid foundation, precept upon precept, line upon line, is a good start and a wise one. We have to start somewhere, and each day we should ask God to direct our steps.

In this chapter, I will briefly discuss twenty steps that, in my experience, I have found to be successful in accomplishing a life of financial freedom. Study them, go over them continuously, and, as much as possible, apply them daily. Then you will be on your way to living a life full of financial freedom.

1. Dedicate Your Life and Your Possessions to God

When you dedicate your life to God and begin to study His Word, He will show you and reveal to you, through His Word, the basic principles of how a *godly* life should be lived, as well as His will for *your* godly life. Dedicating yourself to Him totally and completely opens the door to allow Him to give you understanding in every aspect and every area of life.

In life, there will be challenges and tough decisions to make. There will be tough questions that you will need to ask yourself regarding how to handle certain problems and situations. If you dedicate yourself to God and to learning and understanding His Word, He will reveal the proper godly wisdom to help you become successful in every facet of life that you deal with.

Paul states in Romans 12:1, "I beseech you therefore, brethren, by the mercies of God, that ye present your bodies a living sacrifice, holy, acceptable unto God, which is your reasonable service." Paul continues in verse 2, saying, "And be not conformed to this world: but be ye transformed by the renewing of your mind, that ye may prove what is that good, and acceptable, and perfect, will of God." Once we follow the pattern of the above scripture verses, we will have positioned ourselves to dedicate our lives to God. Seek Him, and through His Word, He will direct your financial path and show you the way to build a solid financial foundation.

On this earth, we use possessions every day. If you have a possession and you love it so much that you are afraid to let go of it if God directs you to do so, then you love it more than you should. Make sure possessions don't possess you; instead, you possess them. In the Bible, the story of the rich young ruler tells us that he was very wealthy (see Luke 18:23). When Jesus told him to sell all that he had, distribute it to the poor, and come, follow Him, the rich ruler was very sorrowful. Obviously, it was very difficult for the rich ruler to give up what he had or what he possessed. In actuality, it seems that his possessions meant more to him than following what Jesus had asked him to do. Any time you have a situation where you are afraid to give up your money, your property, or your prestige when God directs you to, then you are not a candidate for sacrificial living and giving.

For more than twenty years, Abraham trusted and waited on God for the promise that he would bear a son, and God's promise came to pass (see Genesis 21:1–5). After some years had passed, God challenged Abraham to give up his only son as a sacrifice. Pay close attention to the following Bible scenario. This is what happened next:

And Abraham said to his young men, "Stay here with the donkey; the lad and I will go yonder and worship and we will come back to you." So Abraham took the wood of the burnt offering and laid it on Isaac his son; and he took the fire in his hand, and a knife, and the two of them went together. But Isaac spoke to Abraham his father and said, "My father!" And he said, "Here I am, my son." And he said, "Look, the fire and the wood, but where is the lamb for a burnt offering?" And Abraham said, "My son, God will provide for Himself the lamb for a burnt offering." So the two of them went together. Then they came to the place of which God had told him. And Abraham built an altar there and placed the wood in order; and he bound Isaac his son and laid him on the altar, upon the wood. And Abraham stretched out his hand and took the knife to slay his son. But the Angel of the LORD called to him from heaven and said, "Abraham, Abraham!" And he said, "Here I am." And He said, "Do not lay your hand on the lad, or do anything to him; for now I know that you fear God, since you have not withheld your son, your only son, from Me." Then Abraham lifted his eyes and looked, and there behind him was a ram caught in a thicket by its horns. So Abraham went and took the ram, and offered it up for a burnt offering instead of his son. And Abraham called the name of the place, The-Lord-Will-Provide; as it is said to this day, "In the Mount of the Lord it shall be provided." Then the Angel of the Lord called to Abraham a second time out of heaven, and said: "By Myself I have sworn, says the Lord, because you have done this thing, and have not withheld your son, your only son—in blessing I will bless you and in multiplying I will multiply your descendants as the stars of the heaven and as the sand which is on the seashore; and your descendants shall possess the gate of their enemies. In your seed all the nations of the earth shall be blessed, because you have obeyed My voice."

—Genesis 22:5–18, nkjv

Because God is omniscient (all-knowing), He knew what Abraham was going to do before he attempted the sacrifice of his son. Yet because of Abraham's reverence, dedication, and trust in Him, God spared Abraham his son and sent him a lamb to sacrifice instead.

Abraham trusted God, even when he thought the sacrifice was to be his son. This was definitely a demonstration of true dedication. We must learn to put our trust and confidence in God and not in our possessions if we want to experience true, godly financial freedom. As you put God *first*, before your possessions, and follow God's Word and His principles, you are surely to be blessed in many ways.

2. Establish a Budget

A great number of people who hear the word *budget* may have a tendency to think negative thoughts about it or procrastinate when it comes to establishing one. A more positive way to think about it would be to visualize your budget as a *"money management system."* When thinking about creating a money management system, you should have a thought pattern of creating a sense of wealth.

3. Create an Atmosphere of Wealth Around You

One way to create a sense of wealth is by managing your money better. Establishing a budget is what every household should do to maintain or balance their finances and manage their money better. Generally, when formulating a budget for your family, it should be done by using your *net* household income. Some households operate on one salary and others two or more salaries. Generate a plan for what is an appropriate balance for you and your family and *take action toward it*. Make it happen. You have to determine what you want your financial life to be like. Establishing a budget builds the solid foundation needed for good financial management.

My *Financial Freedom Workbook* gives you a complete example and guideline on how to formulate a budget for your household or business. Information on how to receive this workbook is listed in the "Other Books and Materials" section located at the back of this book. Don't hesitate. Start creating your atmosphere of wealth *now.*

4. Start Early

Begin right away to have a mind-set for financial freedom. Take inventory and set priorities, guidelines, and boundaries in your financial arena. *Take the time and initiative to plan/write out your budget immediately.* Habakkuk 2:2 says, "Then the LORD answered me and said: 'Write the vision and make it plain on tablets, that he may run who reads it'" (NKJV). As you can see, the Word of God gives specific instructions concerning getting the vision that you envisioned written down on paper. *Get it accomplished!*

Start a savings account for yourself, even if it means saving and storing your spare, available cash in a cookie jar. For now, *do it.* Remember, don't procrastinate! Don't make excuses or wait for the next promotion, the better job, or the next big break. Start where you are. Do it now!

5. Pay Yourself

Develop a personal regimen in your savings efforts to first pay yourself before spending money on other things. This will automatically produce a form of savings and put you in a habitual mode to save. This will also produce continuity and stability in your savings and how you handle it.

Have you ever heard the expression, "They have money to burn"? Sometimes people spend money needlessly, without purpose, just because they have it. You want to do just the opposite. Hold on to your money and *save, save, save.* Then, when the proper opportunity comes up to invest, spend, bless someone, or give to a charitable cause, you will have what you need when you need it.

Paying yourself first is a simple regimen. When you receive your weekly, biweekly, or monthly income, take or set aside 10 percent for yourself after you pay your tithe (joyfully give 10 percent to God). Remember our first two examples require putting God first. The *first* 10 percent goes to God. The *second* 10 percent that you put aside for yourself is your savings. The rest of your income would be used for your expenditures, bills, etc. *Develop a strong regimen and follow it faithfully.*

6. Get Rich Progressively

When building anything, we have to accomplish it one step at a time. This applies in the area of our finances as well. Doing things one step at a time is a key application in building a financial foundation. If you were training for distance running, it would take hours, days, weeks, and months of workouts and conditioning your body to endure the distance of the race and finish it. Each day, your body will gradually develop into a better state; it will get stronger and stronger. Your ability to run a longer distance will increase little by little with each practice.

This principle is similar when building your wealth. Building a successful financial foundation takes time, training, and patience. It would be advantageous to take the time to study biblical principles on finance. You would need to read and study literature, materials, and books on wealth, investments, and finances.

I would strongly suggest ordering the *Financial Freedom Workbook* and the *Financial Freedom* CD series listed in the back of this book. The *Financial Freedom Workbook* provides a systematic program to follow with action steps to apply. This will help to get you started on a method of continuity and progression. It will create stability for long-term development in building your wealth. Remember, *wealth happens one day at a time.*

7. Be Patient

Do not be too eager and impatient to get rich. As the old saying goes, "Rome was not built in a day." Roman men built it brick by brick, one stone at a time. We must have patience in everything we do in life. Review Hebrews 10:36, which says, "For ye have need of patience, that, after ye have done the will of God, ye might receive the promise."

Think for a moment. If we acquired a very large sum of wealth suddenly, in a very short time, with no training or understanding of how to handle and manage wealth, it probably would not last very long. It would be here today and gone tomorrow, or at least gone in a very short time. Give the process of building your finances some time. Sometimes, because of past decisions, we are faced with the situation of having to pay off huge amounts of debt. In addition, we may have the tendency to feel the need to rush to get out of that debt. Take a step back for a moment and calculate how long it took to get into debt. Be patient and realize that it will take a little time to get out. If you follow godly principles, *you will get out*. Using godly sense to make dollars will bring you out of debt and into your wealthy place.

8. Do Not Gamble Your Wealth Away

From a personal perspective, the lottery is a game of chance, and I don't think Christians should participate. Following God's Word, in my opinion, is a better choice. God gives sound "Word" concerning His financial principles, and there is nothing chancy about it. The lottery game of chance has a luring, seductive spirit of lasciviousness attached to it. It can lure you into playing repeatedly, even when you are losing. Proverbs 13:11 says, "Wealth gotten by vanity shall be diminished: but he that gathereth by labour shall increase." Another translation of the same scripture in Proverbs says, "Wealth from gambling quickly disappears; wealth from hard work grows" (TLB). If we go one step further and take a look at a third translation of the same scripture, it says, "Wealth [not earned but] won in haste or unjustly or from the production of things for vain or detrimental use [such riches] will dwindle away, but he who gathers little by little will increase [his riches]" (AMP). This concept clearly shows that when we are diligent, working earnestly for our wages and consistently saving little by little, our wealth will increase. It takes us back to step seven, which tells us to be patient.

We can use this same concept when trying to decrease our debt. Pay off your credit cards little by little. Paying more than the minimum required each time you make a payment helps to eliminate debt faster. *Do not* continue to use the cards that have reached the maximum credit limit or the cards with the highest interest rates. Stay diligent to this process, and eventually you will pay off those debts. Always keep your focus—and do the same in the spirit realm. Always keep your focus on God and the way He does things and you will never have to worry about playing the games of chance.

9. Spend Less Than You Earn

One of the reasons I chose establishing a budget as one of the twenty steps to financial freedom is because it allows you to know exactly where you are and where you stand in regard to your income each month. You need that in the beginning stages of getting out of debt. A budget is a type of monitoring or checks-and-balances system so that you will know exactly how much you can and cannot spend. This puts you in position to apply the next step: *Spend less than you earn.*

This practice is simple. Always make sure that your expenditures are not more than your earned income. Sometimes we have the tendency to spend more than we earn. This could be a form of temptation, being enticed to have unbalanced wants and desires for material things. More simply expressed, it's called the lust of the eyes. We see many things that we want, but we do not necessarily need them or have to obtain them or have to get them at that exact moment. For example, you decide to go window-shopping when you know that you don't have the extra money in your budget to buy anything. Window-shopping arouses your desire to have the things you see. *Avoid this trap.*

Try to buy only those things that you absolutely need when starting out on your financial plan. Don't go window-shopping. Avoid dinning out when you know you are trying to save. Eat at home. This will help you to spend much less than you normally would.

These are just a few examples of things to avoid when learning to save.

Always try to spend less than you earn. Do not make purchases that you cannot afford, especially credit card purchases. Credit card purchases will only lead to more spending and will then compound into extra debt by increasing the interest and finance charges when you cannot pay the balance in full each month. This takes more money out of your pocket. It affects your finances negatively by taking the flow of money away from you.

Again, *save, save, save.* Start making an effort to spend less than you earn. When you put this basic concept into practice and it becomes a habit in your everyday financial routine of managing your money, then you will surely be on your way to financial freedom.

10. Give the First 10 Percent to God

This step goes back to putting God first in everything in our lives. After all, He is the creator of the heavens, the earth (Gen. 1:1; 2:1–6, NKJV), and humankind (Gen. 2:7–22; Col. 1:15–17, NKJV). God is so gracious. He could have required us to give to Him the first 90 percent while we live on 10 percent. But He didn't. He loves us and cares for us. Putting God first in our financial matters is very important.

Matthew 6:19–34 expresses the importance of not being overly concerned about wealth, food, clothing, or the basic things we need in life (NKJV). Jesus tells us this in Matthew verses 32–33: "For after all these things the Gentiles seek. For your heavenly Father knows that you need all these things. But seek *first* the kingdom of God and His righteousness, and all these things shall be added to you" (emphasis added, NKJV). When we put God first and follow the Word of God and His financial laws and principles, eventually these material things will come to us.

A principle we must follow—that God requires of us—is to give the first 10 percent of all our increase to God. Malachi 3:8–12 tells us about bringing our tithes and why we should do it. It also gives clear details on the results of bringing or paying the tithe (NKJV).

Another example of a man of God bringing his tithes to God can be found in Genesis 28:20–22. Jacob made a vow, saying, "If God will be with me, and keep me in this way that I am going, and give me bread to eat and clothing to put on, so that I come back to my father's house in peace, then the LORD shall be my God. And this stone which I have set as a pillar shall be God's house, and of all that You give me I will surely give a tenth to You" (NKJV). When we apply or carry out this Word from God in our lives, we should expect the results that God promises to come to us.

Following this simple step of giving the first 10 percent of your increase to God is easy. After you receive your weekly, biweekly, or monthly income, take 10 percent of the gross income and set it aside *first*. Before you pay your monthly bills or other expenditures, pay your tithe. The tithe is the first 10 percent of all of your income and increase. Do not fail or fall short in this area of your finances. *Give your tithe to God.*

For example, if your weekly gross salary is $1,000, then the tithe to be given to God is $100. You are probably asking yourself, "How I can give 10 percent to God?" As we learned earlier in this chapter, the Scriptures make reference to bringing the tithes to the storehouse, that there may be food (supply) in God's house (Mal. 3:10, NKJV). Your local storehouse would be your local church. Therefore, you would take your 10 percent out of every weekly, biweekly, or monthly paycheck and take it to the local church that God, through His Holy Spirit, has directed you to become a member of, join membership with, or partner with. For more clarification and reference scriptures on the storehouse being the house of God, refer to 2 Chronicles 31:10–12 and Nehemiah 10:35–39.

Once you begin to act on this step faithfully, you will begin to see the promises that come from following the Word in this matter open up to you. Following this practice will also allow you to gain discipline in your spending and in every area of your financial arena. Leviticus 27:30 clearly states, "And all the tithe of the land, whether of the seed of the land or of the fruit of the tree, is the LORD's. It is holy to the LORD" (NKJV). When we carry out the will of God and do what God instructs us to do, we will have success in life. Tithing is a heart matter, demonstrating we have the heart to please God by doing His will and obeying His Word. If we are willing and obedient to perform His Word, we will eat the good of the land (Isa. 1:19, NKJV).

11. Compound Your Investment Interest

To move ahead in the financial sector, you must diligently try to get rid of ongoing debt. Debt that constantly accrues interest and finance charges is money moving away from you and not flowing in-stream toward building your financial assets or your financial portfolio. Try as much as possible to consolidate debts and work from a plan, as this will allow a lower interest rate and lower finance charges. If possible, try to consolidate and pay off as much of your current debt that you can, especially when there is a 0 percent interest-rate option available. Work with creditors to settle debts with a compromise payment of less than the total amount due. This will allow you to save money by eliminating the responsibility to pay the total amount of the original debt.

Begin to look for additional possibilities for new wealth to come into your life. Find new ways to use your money each month when debts are paid off to build your wealth and increase your net worth. This will be the perfect opportunity to start investing in certificates of deposits, mutual funds, bonds, securities, money-market funds, or trust funds—in other words, investments that will yield interest.

12. Use IRAs and Other Tax-Deferred Investments

Once your debt is paid, this will open up an availability of money for you to invest in other areas to bring in other streams of income and build your financial portfolio. Before you start investing in other areas, determine that you have considerable savings and enough in your savings account for emergencies. Make sure you are investing in the "known" first.

The "known" are things such as your mortgage, insurance, transportation expenses, and other daily living expenses and responsibilities. These liabilities provide security for you and your family. A few other "knowns" are medical expenses, day care for the children, and educational expenses for the entire family. These are basic living responsibilities that you know you will have to provide for your family or yourself. Once these responsibilities are fulfilled, then you can invest in the "unknown," or secondary investments.

"Unknown" investments would be stocks, bonds, commodities, securities, and market trading. Some degree of risk is involved in these investments. Good secondary investments are tax-deferred or tax-exempt investments. Pay yourself by opening up an IRA. An IRA (individual retirement account) is a great tax-deferred investment. These types of accounts provide tax benefits to you, the holder.

A few common types of IRAs are:

§ Traditional: Tax-deferred benefit; allows a 2K—5K investment per person.

§ Roth: First became available in 1998; offers more flexibility than the traditional IRA; earnings can accumulate tax-free forever; available to a larger segment of the public with income limits.

These investments promote more ways to withdraw funds without penalties.

When deciding to start making secondary investments, first consult with other family members who would be involved in the decision making process. Remember to use good business sense and wisdom. *Wise people listen to good information.* Gaining your financial freedom is all about using sense to make dollars—good godly sense, that is.

13. Wait Before You Buy a Car

In general, purchasing a car for our families or ourselves is something just about all of us have to do at some point in our lives. The first bit of advice to take before making this decision is to educate yourself on consumer interest and interest rates. The larger your down payment, the less you will have to finance, and that means a smaller loan with smaller payments and lower finance and interest rates.

The ultimate scenario would be to pay cash for your

automobile and not have a car payment, but we are not all in the financial position to do so. Another route to take would be to purchase a used, lower-priced vehicle instead of a new vehicle and be able to pay cash for the less expensive purchase. This would again avoid high interest rates, financing, and car payments. The money that would have been used for car payments can then go into a savings account.

If deciding to buy a used vehicle, review the blue book—a manual that gives a fair market price or estimated value for a used vehicle depending on its year and mileage (see www.kbb.com). The Internet provides many ways to save with online purchases. Shop online and pay less interest.

There are many things to consider when purchasing your vehicle. If you are deciding to buy a new vehicle, check to see what the current Lemon Law states. Also count the costs involved when purchasing a vehicle. This would include insurance, maintenance and upkeep, mileage, gas costs, and the like. Before making a final decision, always check to see if negotiations are possible. Select the vehicle best suited to your budget. This will allow you to enjoy your vehicle and take care of it properly. Implementing routine car maintenance will give you years of trouble-free performance and take you through the long-term. Remember to be content where you are now, and God will increase you as you follow His Word.

14. Stay Out of Debt

This is so important. When developing a plan to stay out of debt, be sure not to overstep the boundaries of your income. Determine that you have made a solid, realistic budget (money management plan) and submit, follow, and stick to it like glue. Be consistent with this plan. Constantly review your spending plan, and stay focused. Prepare yourself mentally to spend wisely and honestly. Connect with God; seek Him, even in your spending. *Only purchase what you really need.*

You do not want to get yourself back into debt again and go backward. You want to continue to move forward in this area. Stay away from and avoid unnecessary loans. The Word tells us that we should be lenders and not borrowers (Deut. 28:12, NKJV). Once you pay off your credit card(s) and loan debts, do not fall back into that trap. When you must use your credit card, always pay off the total balance with each month's payment.

Handle your household finances like a prosperous business. Analyze your unplanned trips to the ATM. Balance your checkbook daily, and reconcile your checkbook monthly. Review bank-imposed expenses and fees. Protect yourself from overdraft.

Keep your faith in God, and focus on His Word. He will give you the courage and the confidence to accomplish this goal and be successful in your finances. When Joshua followed the Word of the Lord, meditating continually on it day and night, he became strong and courageous and accomplished his goal, and so can you (see Joshua 1:6–9, NKJV).

15. Minimize Risk by Diversifying

In life, there is a balance in everything, and this pertains to our finances as well. As you build your financial portfolio, don't put all of your eggs in one basket, as the saying goes. *Diversify your investments.*

When gaining and maintaining your financial freedom, have a variety of investments in your portfolio. Divide your investments and liabilities among different investment companies. Channel your investments into more than one stream. When you start investing and diversifying your financial portfolio, always do your research. Learn the language of investing.

There are many options here. For example, if you decide to invest in government securities, you'll find there are several types. Here is a short list of government securities: treasury bills, notes and bonds, zero-coupon treasuries (STRIPS), US government agency securities, and others. There are many choices. Do your research, and choose wisely.

16. Minimize Losses, Maximize Gains

While building your wealth, always let your actions be smart choices. Seek to make wise decisions each step of the way. This will help you to avoid losses and eliminate setbacks. Pay attention to investments that you made that are bringing in high yields and making profits. Focus on those particular types of investments to increase your wealth. Learn from your mistakes, and avoid loss in the future. Continue your research as much as possible. Observe the economy for inflation and other tip-offs before making decisions that involve large sums of money. Be a continuous note-taker and resource-reader. Break the bad habits that take away from your financial gain, and develop the skills that allow you to increase financially and live in financial freedom.

17. Protect Your Wealth With Insurance

Protect your assets! As your wealth grows, you will begin to accumulate assets. You will want to feel comfortable and secure, knowing that if some unforeseen circumstance happens to you or your family, your assets would be protected. This is why it is very important to have insurance. Make sure that you have insurance on all the basics: your home, your properties, your car, your investments, your financial accounts, etc.

In addition, it is always important to have a will, so that in the event of death, you would have everything protected and in order. Your will should also note an executor, a person or persons put in charge who would oversee your businesses, corporations, estates, assets, properties, trust funds, and whatever else is necessary.

Do not fail to do this. You would not want everything that you have worked so hard for and labored to build to be lost and put in the hands of irresponsible persons. As testator, you want to ensure that the executor has specific instructions and directions on how your estate should be handled. As you age, you will want to set many things in order. *Be responsible, and insure your assets.*

18. Consider Charitable Giving

One of the quickest ways to build your wealth is to give. One of God's principles on giving in the Bible tells us that if we sow sparingly, we will reap sparingly, and if we sow bountifully, we will reap bountifully (2 Cor. 9:6, NKJV). The next part of that principle says, "So let each one give as he purposes in his heart, not grudgingly or of necessity; for God loves a cheerful giver" (v. 7, NKJV). *Honor God with a worthy seed.* The Scriptures clearly admonish us to be cheerful givers. For instance, let's look at verse 8, which describes one of the promises that comes to us as a result of our giving: "And God is able to make all grace abound toward you, that you, always having all sufficiency in all things, may have an abundance for every good work" (NKJV). God wants to make sure that we have enough when we do good works.

Charitable giving is pleasing to God. Take the opportunity to do something good. Charitable giving not only helps others, but it is also a wise investment for the giver. As you give bountifully to charity, you will reap bountifully. Make the effort to not only give your finances, but also your skills and your time. Volunteer to help at local charitable organizations.

19. Set Short-Term Financial Goals

Be sure to set short-term goals for yourself in your quest to build wealth. This will allow you to continue to move forward one step at a time. A simple short-term goal is to continue to have gainful employment (employment that brings in income) to consistently provide for the needs of yourself and your family. See your employment income as providing seed to sow. Provision to sow seeds presents the opportunity to give. Remember, God loves a cheerful giver! Continue to improve your skills, and continue your education. Take a few minutes twice a week to listen to or read some kind of financial information. Compare what you hear and read to God's Word, and follow godly wisdom. These are just a few suggestions of short-term goals. The key point is to keep moving ahead into financial freedom.

20. Set Long-Term Financial Goals

Take inventory of your financial priorities. Decide where, in the next five or ten years from now, you want to be financially. Write your goals down, and review them continually. Keep the dream in front of you so you can see it. Envision what you want your financial portfolio to look like in five to ten years. Trust God to give you creative ideas and inventions that will increase your wealth. Plan and outline future creative ventures that will produce income. Continue to create an atmosphere of wealth all around you. Remember to set goals that can help others as well. Continue to use sense to make dollars—godly sense, that is!

Chapter Two

SEVEN LAWS
OF INCREASE

IIIIIIIIIIIIIIIIIIIIIIIIIIIIIIIIIIII

T HERE ARE MANY ways you can increase your finances. In this chapter, we will review seven basic laws of increase.

Before we go into these laws, let's look at what the phrase *financial debt* means. Before we increase, we need to first get out of debt. A simple definition that I have for financial debt is *spending money that you don't have, making decisions that prefabricate who you really are, being stuck in financial bondage and prison with no release date, and carrying financial insecurity and fear about your future comfort.* Who wants to be in bondage and in prison and not know when they are going to get out? None of God's children need to be entangled in this sort of uncertainty.

Now, let us look at the definition of *financial freedom*. Financial freedom is *spending money that will create harmony in your life, making decisions knowing who you really are, gaining freedom from an unbalanced financial scale, resting in financial security, and experiencing peace regarding your future comfort and supply.*

Two prevalent contrasts between the two definitions are: 1) Financial freedom is knowing who you really are, and financial debt is prefabricating who you are; and 2) Financial freedom brings peace while financial debt breeds fear. Who wants fear in their life? I think we all would like to have peace instead of fear.

Let's set a foundation and a track record with a few scriptures to show that God is a God who wants and desires to increase and prosper us. Not only because of the financial systems of our world do we want to be financially free from debt, but God also wants us to be free from debt. Even in relationship with our fellow man, God does not want us to be in debt, as it states in Romans 13:8: "Keep out of debt and owe no man anything, except to love one another; for he who loves his neighbor [who practices loving others] has fulfilled the Law [relating to one's fellowmen, meeting all its requirements]" (AMP).

Proverbs 10:22 states, "The blessing of the LORD, it maketh rich, and he addeth no sorrow with it." I want to make it very clear and convince you that God wants us to prosper and increase. He does not want us weighed down with the bondage of financial debt. He wants us to experience financial freedom and prosperity.

To continue to reinforce that God wants us to prosper and increase, let's review Proverbs 13:22: "A good man leaveth an inheritance to his children's children: and the wealth of the sinner is laid up for the just." That means wealth is sitting there, waiting for those of us who have been justified by God to get hold of it. It is sitting there—we have to go after it, we have to get it, we have to claim it, and we have to possess it. (See also Ecclesiastes 2:26.)

Understand this. When someone says you have been given something, that is one thing. To possess what you have been given, that is a totally different thing. You could be given something and not possess it. You could have it sitting on your dresser but not have it in your hand. You have to possess what God has given to you. That is the difference between people who know what God says is available and people who are actually walking in what God says is available.

Let's look at another scripture. Psalm 68:19 says, "Blessed be the Lord, who daily loadeth us with benefits, even the God of our salvation. Selah." *Daily* means every day. Every day God piles us up with benefits, even the God of our salvation. If you are saved by God, or have received salvation, He is the God of your salvation. The Bible says He daily, every day, piles us up and loads us with benefits. Benefits are things that are good for us, advantageous to us, and helpful to us. God is always providing things that are helpful for us. That's what He desires to do.

Some people think God wants to condemn us. However, according to John 3:17, Jesus said, "For God sent not His son into the world to condemn the world; but that the world through him might be saved." Therefore, it is God's desire to save us and get us out of trouble. It is God's desire to deliver us and make us whole. He daily loads us up with His benefits, but we have to accept what He gives us and walk into what He has for us.

I want to continue to establish that it is truly God's desire and will that the people who serve Him, love Him, live for Him, and honor Him would increase, prosper, and not be in financial bondage or financial prison. Proverbs 8:21 says this: "That I may cause those that love me to inherit substance; and I will fill their treasures." *Substance* in this scripture refers to things that you can feel—material things. As Christians, we are not materialistic people. In other words, material things are not our number-one desire or our main focus or primary aim in life. But God does desire that His people have substance—that we have materials we live with that we can use to support our families, the gospel, and ourselves. That is His will. That's His desire.

Jesus said this in John 10:10: "The thief cometh not, but for to steal, and to kill, and to destroy: I am come that they might have life, and that they might have it more abundantly." He desires for us to have superabundant life. Proverbs 8:21 also says, "I will fill their treasures." God wants us to have treasures, and He does not want our treasures to be empty. God desires to fill our treasures.

The final scripture I want to mention in our foundation for building the case that God wants us to prosper is 3 John 1:2, which states this: "Beloved, I wish above all things that thou mayest prosper and be in health, even as thy soul prospereth." Our soul involves our mind, our will, our intellect, and our emotions. So as our mind changes and gets renewed to the ways of God and the things of God as described in His Word, then our soul prospers. We begin to know what God wants for us through His Word. God wants us to increase materially. He wants us to increase in substance. He wants us to increase in wellness, in wholeness, and in health. He wants us to be well-rounded people who represent Him in the earth.

We have reviewed several scriptures that show God wants us to increase and prosper. There are numerous scriptures in the Bible that talk about increase and wealth and what God has available and wants for His people. We won't be able to cover them all, but we can gather the point being made from the scriptures already mentioned in this section that God wants His people to prosper and increase. God wants us blessed. He wants us to increase, to prosper, and to be out of financial bondage. God shows us in His Word that He wants us to be elevated, on top, and blessed (see Deuteronomy 28:1–13).

Another quick point I want to mention is that *we do not serve God because of what He can do for us, but because we love Him.* If we had nothing, we should still love, serve, and honor God. As we learned earlier, He also wants us to be givers. When we give to help others, we should have confidence in God to know that He will bless us again. When we are obedient to His Word in our giving, He blesses and increases us. Always have a heart to serve and honor God, no matter what circumstances surround your life.

Before I begin to reveal the seven laws of increase, I want to go over the definition of money. Money is a medium, or tool, of exchange for goods, services, and the necessities of life. Money is also known as currency, cash, or liquid resources. It is clearly defined as *a tool to obtain material goods, as well as a means to achieve fulfillment and pleasure for oneself and others.* Money should not be used only to obtain things for yourself, but to help others as well. We use money to execute what needs to be accomplished in the earth. God gave humankind dominion over the earth (Gen. 1:26). He wants us to use what we have to help dominate, supply, and support the earth.

Now let's focus our attention on the seven laws of increase. I'm sure there are more than seven laws that pertain to increase, but these seven are the ones I want to discuss.

Law 1: Free your consciousness and develop good money habits. Renew your perspective to think God first, people second, then money and things.

First, if we do not have our thinking prioritized according to the order of the first law in terms of rank and importance, then we need to renew our minds and change our thinking. We should get our consciousness in line with the perspective that God is first, people are second, money is third, and things are fourth.

Human life, the life of humanity, is more important than making lots of money and more money. Don't misunderstand me; we do need to make money. As we reviewed earlier, there is nothing wrong with having a lot of money. We just need to get the right perspective about money and financial freedom—what they mean and exactly how they should be balanced with the other things that are important in life. Money should never mean more to you than God or people. The scripture reveals that God, our Creator, is the one who gives us the power to get wealth (Deut. 8:11–18, NKJV). Understanding that will allow you to put the concept of money in proper perspective and not let it rule and reign over you. It must never take first place before God or the care and concern for people, the human race.

Money is something that has to be managed properly, just like anything else in life. Money is a basic tool in life that we use for exchange, and we need to accept that. We have the responsibility to manage what we earn properly so that it serves and meets our financial needs and other basic needs in life.

First, we need to search within ourselves to find out how we really feel about money. Analyze your attitude about and toward money. Do you feel bad about having a lot of money? Are you embarrassed because you may have a lot of money or not enough money? Are you afraid or ashamed that people know you have or don't have a lot of money? Do you think it is OK to have a lot of money? Are you afraid to let people know that you want or desire to increase in your finances? Do you think poverty is next to godliness? Are you self-conscious about what people think about you, your money, and your financial status?

There could be many issues going on concerning your attitude toward money. We have to get a good consciousness about finances. We have to understand that money is simply a basic tool that we use to meet our daily needs. The first law is all about getting our minds and our consciousness set right about money. We have to get comfortable with finances and the subject of finances and money, and not have a fear of them.

One of the scriptures in the Bible talks about the love of money being the root of all evil (1 Tim. 6:10). Have you ever heard someone referring to this scripture and quoting it as "Money is the root of all evil"? That is not what the scripture says. Money is not evil, and money is not the root of evil. The root of all evil, in terms of money, is when people think selfishly and wrongly about money—when they love money more than they love people and more than they love God. Some people seek after finances, money, and increase more than they seek after God. It is that kind of erotic, *eros* love toward money that is evil. It causes people to do all kinds of things. It causes people to sin, to cheat, to lie, to scheme, to walk on others, to put each other down, to commit murder, to abuse others, and much more. It's the *love* of money that promotes and provokes these kinds of actions, and that is what is evil. But money itself is just paper. It's currency. It's a tool that we use, and when we think of it that way, we will put it in its proper perspective. Then money can be a help to us when it is managed properly and not loved and used in an abusive manner to do the wrong things.

Law 2: Tell the truth; stop lying about your money. Will the real you please stand up?

There used to be a game show called *To Tell the Truth*. They would always plant two imposters in the game session with the real candidate. At the end of each session, they would ask the real candidate to stand up. Well, the second law of increase is all about telling the truth—the truth about your money and financial status.

Will the real you please stand up? What do I mean by this? We must admit to ourselves where we really are in our financial status and tell the truth. I have found that lying about who you are takes money away from you. When you tell the truth about your finances, it adds to you.

Let me try to explain what I mean. Lying can destroy the flow of money in your life. Why? Because when you lie about who you are, you will overspend and buy things you cannot afford. You will do things you should not do concerning your finances to make a presentation of yourself that is really not you. It's not where you really stand financially. You'll charge purchases to your credit cards, thereby resulting in credit card debt. You may dine out at expensive restaurants that you can't really afford because you want to make it appear or look as though you are financially able. When friends ask you to go out and you don't want it to seem as though you cannot afford it, you'll accompany them. As a result, you spend money that you don't have. This would be considered the same as lying about who you are and your financial status. The honest response would be to say, "I can't fit that into my budget this week, so I'll have to decline your invitation this time." This sort of response would add to you, because this would allow you not to overspend or spend money that is not available in your budget.

Deciding to take action by doing things you cannot afford creates taxation on money that you shouldn't be spending, and finance charges are added to your bill on the credit card you should not have used in the first place. Therefore, this kind of practice takes the flow of money away from you. It's taking money out of your pocket because you are not being honest about who you are or your financial situation.

The second law is about being honest about who you are and your financial status. Don't lie to yourself and others. Pride causes us to respond this way. People make purchases they cannot afford and, in many cases, lose the purchase and the money used to acquire the purchase.

An example of this is as follows. A consumer purchases something on credit or obtains a loan to purchase something. Because the promised payment schedule was not met, the creditors have the option to come and take repossession of the merchandise. The consumer purchased something they could not afford and could not maintain the payments. Therefore, the money that was already invested in the purchase of the product was lost due to repossession by the creditors. Again, this takes money out of your pocket when you are not honest about your finances. It takes the flow of money away from you. Just be honest. Honesty is the best policy.

Don't be too concerned about other people. Other people do not define us. How they think and feel about us (contrary to God's Word) does not define who we are. We don't define ourselves by that. Who and what God says we are defines us. Proverbs 16:18 says, "Pride goeth before destruction, and a haughty spirit before a fall." You do not want to let pride and a lack of will and constitution define who you are and affect the flow of money in your life.

There are too many people overburdened with credit card debt for the wrong reasons. Sometimes we have to use our credit cards in major jams and emergency situations. However, just to use them for the sake of going on an impulse shopping spree because of some whimsical fantasy is irresponsible, and it starts the process of being overburdened with credit card debt. This puts you in a financial bondage that you do not want in your life. Getting out of debt can be very difficult. *Avoid credit card debt if possible!*

Falling into error with this law, which is not being who you are and not letting the real you be seen, can result in emotional insecurity and strained relationships. When money becomes scarce, relationships may become bad or strained. We can begin to relate to people differently, even those that we love and care for. We start being offensive to and offended by people for no reason. We may become short-tempered with people. A lot of the troubles and the problems that we experience in our marriages, in our relationships, and in other areas of our lives in our short-temperedness may be due to our lack of financial discipline resulting in financial bondage and financial prison. This can sometimes bring on a feeling of entrapment, so we may have a tendency to retaliate on others and think that it is always someone else's fault. Someone else is always the reason we made the decision that we made. No—we chose to do what we did, and we have to accept our erroneous choices. We cannot blame our mistakes on other people. We must guard against this, and the best way to eliminate this is to just be honest. We have to admit when we can't afford to do some things.

Take another alternative and do things that are affordable for your budget. Take a walk in the park. Get a nice DVD of your choice and sit at home and watch it or enjoy it with your family. Plant a garden together, or spend some family time together. There are many similar alternatives to take. These are just a few. Be comfortable and at peace with one another until your finances begin to increase and begin to grow. Do not get discouraged. Remain content. You do not have to prove anything to anybody or anyone.

God gives us pictures and examples of people who are increasing and prospering. These are good pictures. We can keep them as a mental example, paste them on our walls, and keep focus on them as our next goal or the next step in our process to gaining financial freedom. These pictures are things that we can work toward, but that doesn't mean we have to be at that level tomorrow. Financial progress takes time. You do not know how long the person in your example has been sowing seeds and following principles of increase in order to get to the place where they are today.

Instead of taking the systematic process to reach those goals, we run after all kinds of things. We leave locales, we go here, we go there, trying to find a difference in our lives, trying to find something that will cause us to catapult into what we think is increase and victory. We go to another city, and we still have not resolved the problem. The problem is on the inside of us. Will the *real you* please stand up?

Let's be honest with who we are. As we learned earlier, God's system is progressive. His system takes us from one level to the next, one stage to the next. You are not supposed to be the same person as your mentor or the same person as your role model. We are constantly learning from them. Your mentor is a guiding example of where you can go as you continuously practice the laws of increase.

Every now and then, we misunderstand and think, "Well, if that's where they are, I should be in the same position as they're in now." No. That is not how the progressive process and plan works. For example, if you have a baby this week and someone else has a baby ten months from now, the baby born ten months later is not going to be as progressed as the baby born ten months earlier. It would be unfair to expect the latter child to be at the same level of progression as the former child. We have to realize where we are in life, who we are in life, and what our plan is in life and then establish our plan and work toward it.

Law 3: Make the decision to move from the past. Let it go!

You have to make a decision to let go of the past. Just let it go. What do I mean by letting it go and moving from the past? Some of the things that we have to deal with in life are inward issues. When we deal with the inward us, then the outward manifestation will result in growth and increase. This outward growth will be done correctly and done well in the scheme of God's plans. This means looking at what you have and not at what you had.

From time to time, our situations and circumstances change in life. In addition, some may find themselves stuck and unable to move ahead because they see themselves as they once were. Well, the situation has changed now. You are not who and what you used to be at this point or juncture in life. Perhaps you don't have what you used to have. So, examine your situation and be real, up-front, and honest with yourself.

Maybe at one time in your life, you did make a six-digit figure. Possibly things could have happened, whatever the course life took, and it brought change to your circumstances. Well, if you no longer earn a six-digit salary and your income is considerably less, then you cannot live as if you're still earning that six-digit salary. There is nothing wrong with downsizing; there is nothing wrong with making the change.

I promise you that when you do it and you stay with the rules, principles, concepts, and precepts of God, without a doubt, you are going to progress and increase, because God is a God of increase. We learned this earlier in our text. God wants to multiply; He doesn't want to subtract from us. If you stick with His principles, you are going to increase. However, if you continue spending as though you are living on a six-digit salary and you're not, then you will spend money that you don't have, getting yourself deeper and deeper into a hole of financial debt, possibly with no way out. Do not put yourself in this position. *Do it God's way.* Follow His principles and guidelines.

Have you ever known anyone who lost everything they had and yet they still wanted to live on Park Avenue? They still wanted to act as if they could shop at Saks Fifth Avenue? They still wanted to spend money that they didn't have? By doing this, they hurt their family's progress as well as their own. This is being selfish, and it is one of the results, or outcome, of falling into the love-of-money trap. This is not the love of God. God's love is not selfish. Follow God's way and make progress. Do not regress.

Let's take a look at Psalm 66:10–12, for it says, "For thou, O God, hast proved us: thou hast tried us, as silver is tried. Thou broughtest us into the net; thou laidest affliction upon our loins. Thou hast caused men to ride over our heads; we went through fire and through water: but thou broughtest us out into a wealthy place." In other words, we have gone through many things in our lives. We have had bosses and leaders. We've gone through the fire and through the water. We went through all of those things, but God has brought us out of it all into a wealthy place. There is no way that you can serve God, live for God, trust God, love God, and not get into your wealthy place. Not all of us are going to have the same level of wealth, which is obvious, but we will all have our wealthy place. Our place where there is more than enough.

God is El Shaddai, the God of more than enough. Why is He the God of more than enough? He is the God of more than enough because God wants you to have enough to take care of you and have some left to invest in other people. He also wants you to have enough to carry out His good will and plans in the earth. He wants you to have more than you need for yourself. If you don't have more than you need for yourself, you cannot help anyone else.

Sometimes we get our spiritual consciousness wrong and think God does not want us to pay our mortgage or take our family on vacations. Well, do we have a God that is concerned about every area of our lives? Do we serve a God that really wants those things for you and me? God wants you to be able to pay your mortgage; He wants you to be able to take your family on vacation; and He wants you to have enough for every good cause. He wants you to be able to give to the church building program, help the homeless, and give charitable donations; all are good causes. He is the God of more than enough. You and I, as believers, should have enough to give to every good cause.

The Bible tells us in the book of 2 Corinthians that He gives seed to the sower. He gives us bread to eat, He gives us seed to sow, and He gives us enough to give to other people so that our righteousness is seen (2 Cor. 9:9–15, NKJV). How is our righteousness seen? Our righteousness is seen when we are able to help someone else. For example, if someone is about to have their electricity turned off because of non-payment, you can step in and help them by paying the bill. They would see the righteousness and the fruit of God in your life by your doing so. You have more than enough to pay your own electric bill, and now you can help someone else.

That is where God wants us to be. However, given that we have gotten ourselves in so much debt by trying to keep up with the Joneses and we have gotten ourselves in such an excess of expenditures, trying to keep up with those around us, we do not have more than enough left over to help someone else.

Isaiah 1:19 says, "If ye be willing and obedient, ye shall eat the good of the land." In my opinion, I think what God is saying to us is that whatever land you find yourself in, you will be able to eat the good of that land. Sometimes we think that eating the good of the land means we are supposed to eat the good of the millionaires' land. It simply means you are to eat the good of the land wherever you are at that designated time in your life.

If you are willing and obedient to God's Word, He will take care of you. For example, you may be in a particular community. In that community, you should have the best of the best. As you progress and increase in that community, you will outgrow it. In addition, you will have enough to move to another community, an upgraded one. Then while you are there, you will progress and eat the good of the land in that community. It does not mean that you are supposed to jump from a community that you can afford to one that you can't afford just because you do not want the real you to stand up. *We have to learn the sound principles of the Word of God.* We have to learn God's process. Get in touch with your outlook on finances, your outlook on your dreams, and your outlook on your wishes and your visions. God wants us to have dreams. He wants us to have visions. He wants us to have things that we are pursuing in life, and He wants us to increase in life. God wants us to anticipate great things. It is a step-by-step process. God will ultimately bring us into our wealthy place one step at a time and one day at a time.

Wealth happens one day at a time. It doesn't just happen overnight. Proverbs 13:11 says, "Wealth [not earned but] won in haste or unjustly or from the production of things for vain or detrimental use [such riches] will dwindle away, but he who gathers little by little will increase [his riches]" (AMP). When you get wealth through the get-rich-quick process or in other ways, such as the lottery, gambling, and things that do not produce morality or a good, upstanding life and character in the lives of people, that kind of wealth will diminish.

For example, you play the slot machine or black-jack in Las Vegas and you suddenly win a lot of money. Usually that money will quickly diminish. Why? Because most times, the winner does not have the character, the principles, or the godly precepts to maintain that kind of financial increase. For instance, it has been found, after tracking the lives of those who have won the lottery after a year or two, that around that period or timeframe, they are broke and have lost all their winnings. They usually spend the money frivolously; it is not managed properly. They only have short-term goals and typically do not know how to maintain finances. Their money quickly diminishes.

The last part of Proverbs 13:11 states that he who gathers little by little will increase. When you acquire little by little, along the way you learn the principles of gaining, maintaining, and keeping what you have. When you learn the principle of a thing, in this case finances, you learn the proper thing to do with what you have. For example, some athletes and entertainers acquire considerably large amounts of wealth very quickly, and when their careers are done, they have very little wealth left. This happens sometimes because no one has taught them to understand basic financial principles. No one has helped them understand how to keep what they have, share what they have, invest what they have, and manage what they have acquired. You learn

daily, step-by-step. I encourage you to get these principles and laws that we have discussed in your spirit, your
heart, and your life. When you do, you'll know how to
keep the wealth you gain. You will know what God says
about it.

Determine how you want your own financial life
to be. *Get disciplined, and get started.* Make it happen.
When you run a marathon, you have to train for a long
time. It takes training, and it takes a lot of work. You
have to discipline not only your mind, but your body as
well. You have to build your muscles, your stamina, and
your total body. Building your financial empire is much
the same. It will not be a sprint run. It will be a marathon. It will take time, energy, and effort to build your
finances. A marathon takes endurance to the end. We
must have the same spirit of endurance when building
our wealth and moving ahead to financial freedom.

Create a sense of wealth by managing money better.
Create a sense of wealth even when you don't have
the wealth yet. Think like a wealthy person. Create
the sense of wealth around you. You have to use your
thinking abilities. Proverbs 8:12 says, "I wisdom dwell
with prudence, and find out knowledge of witty inventions." God gives us creativity. He will give you what it
takes to have creative ideas to invent different things
and come up with different things that will help you
and your family to create wealth in your life. True
wealth is not always seen, because true wealth happens
on the inside first; then it manifests itself on the outside.

In the Book of Philippians, Paul said, "Brethren, I count not myself to have apprehended: but this one thing I do, forgetting those things which are behind, and reaching forth unto those things which are before, I press toward the mark for the prize of the high calling of God in Christ Jesus" (Phil. 3:13–14). Paul had a specific goal; he focused on it, he left the past in the past, and he did not look back. So, look at what you have and not at what you had. Get out of your past, and look toward your future. Don't talk about what and who you once were. Focus on the here and now. *Today will take you to tomorrow.*

Law 4: Learn what is right for you and your family, and take action toward it. Make a plan. Write a budget. Invest in the "known" first.

The foundation to financial freedom is a spending plan. Establish a budget for you and your family. Defeat financial emergencies by building a "safe net" income. This will help you avoid putting yourself in a financial dilemma. Ephesians 4:27 states, "Leave no [such] room or foothold for the devil [give no opportunity to him]" (AMP). When the enemy, the adversary, finds an open door where he can come in and cause havoc, he will try to come in. You need to prepare yourself ahead of time by creating a budget that works for you and your family, and you must remain faithful to it. Therefore, when the adversary tries to attack you in the area of your finances, he has no room or foothold to enter that area.

As you use your "sense," stick to your budget, and make sure that you care for your family to the best of your knowledge, God will partner with you in this. When you are a tither, and the devourer tries to come in, the Bible says in Malachi 3:11, "And I will rebuke the devourer for your sakes, and he shall not destroy the fruits of your ground; neither shall your vine cast her fruit before the time in the field, saith the Lord of hosts." As you stick to your plan, you will be able to save. In addition, when financial emergencies come up, you will have more than enough to meet your needs. This will eliminate many problems, and you will defeat the adversary if he tries to attack you in the area of your finances. Praise God for His provision!

You have to plan. *We have to plan not to fail.* You cannot spend everything you make. God is giving you wisdom, insight, and knowledge through His Word. He shows you how to handle your affairs so that you can resist the adversary. It is totally up to you. God has given us everything that we need. In this fourth law of increase, the proper budget is a key factor in moving toward your financial freedom. Go back and review this topic in chapter one.

Commit to a realistic spending plan. Pay careful attention to your daily spending. Try to handle your household finances like a prosperous business. Put your budget on paper, write it down, start it, and submit to it.

You have to have ownership and get control over your money. This means securing gainful employment to provide the finances that you need daily to meet the daily needs for yourself and your family. There is an order to everything that we do. Paul talks about this order and of following the example of the apostles even in our work ethic. Paul and the apostles worked hard for their food and needs so they would not be a burden to anyone:

> For you yourselves know how you ought to follow us, for we were not disorderly among you; nor did we eat anyone's bread free of charge, but worked with labor and toil night and day, that we might not be a burden to any of you, not because we do not have authority, but to make ourselves an example of how you should follow us.
>
> For even when we were with you, we commanded you this: If anyone will not work, neither shall he eat. For we hear that there are some who walk among you in a disorderly manner, not working at all, but are busybodies. Now those who are such we command and exhort through our Lord Jesus Christ that they work in quietness and eat their own bread.
> —2 THESSALONIANS 3:7–12, NKJV

We all need a job. Even the scriptures above tell us that if we don't work, we don't eat. Of course, I am referring to people who are able bodied. People who are capable of working should be working. You do not need to be a liability in the body of Christ. You need to work and bring in the proper amount of income to be able to handle your affairs. The Word of God says we need to work. Sometimes the state of the economy and the competitiveness of the job market will not allow us to secure a job in our trained or degreed field, and this may require us to take a job in other career areas. It may also require us to sometimes take a job that we are overqualified for. Nevertheless, do not let this discourage you. Press forward and follow God's plan. Be faithful in the job that you have, and if you are diligent, God will increase and promote you. We can be reminded of this in Hebrews 11:6, which says, "But without faith it is impossible to please him: for he that cometh to God must believe that he is, and that he is a rewarder of them that diligently seek him."

If you follow the Word, the precepts, and concepts of God, you are going to increase. Keep your character, attitude, and work ethic in order and in line with God's standards, and you will see increase and promotion in your life. Wait patiently with faith and expectation. Psalm 37:34 states, "Wait for and expect the Lord and keep and heed His way, and He will exalt you to inherit the land; [in the end] when the wicked are cut off you shall see it" (AMP). Have confidence in your God, and know who you are in Christ. You have to be serious about living your life God's way, according to His Word. Even if you cannot get your dream job at this time, be realistic enough to know that you do need a job. Securing steady, gainful employment will allow you to provide, prepare, and take care of yourself, your family, and your financial responsibilities. It will also provide a seed to start your sowing. Remember, *you can only grow a harvest if a seed is planted in the ground.*

Financial responsibilities require setting priorities in life. If you are head of the household and you want to go back to school to secure a better job with a higher income bracket to make better provision for your family, that is a great idea. You may have a certain dream occupation or career that you have wanted to pursue. This is great, but you cannot neglect other responsibilities to do this. Your priorities must be in order. Put first things first. You cannot just quit your current job to pursue these dreams. You have to continue to meet the financial needs and responsibilities of your family. You could possibly take some courses part-time, in the evening, working toward that goal and completing it one step at a time. This would allow you to pursue the goal and meet your financial needs and responsibilities. The latter mentioned is the better course. This would be the right way to do it and still live life successfully.

We have to live life according to God's standards and truths. God will partner with us. He wants us to keep our dreams alive and pursue them. Don't let your dreams die. Keep them alive. Think about your dreams, talk about them, meditate on them, go after them, and find ways to accomplish them. However, maintain a realistic livelihood through gainful employment while you're pursuing your dream. As you are keeping your dream alive, it will happen for you. It will come to pass because that is God's desire for you. Psalm 37:4 tells us this: "Delight yourself also in the Lord, and He shall give you the desires of your heart" (NKJV). God knows that you have a dream. He wants it to happen for you. Put God as your first priority. Continue to pursue Him and His principles, and His way of doing things will cause your dreams to manifest.

Finally, invest in the "known" first. Known investments are those things that you know you are liable for. These are your basic necessities and responsibilities. Again, some examples of this would be your rent, mortgage, electric bill, utility bills, food, groceries, car payment, insurance, phone expenses, medical bills, school funds, day care, educational expenses, etc. Also, make sure you have a basic savings account. This would be a simple known investment where there is no risk involved. Always cover your known investments before you invest in the unknown.

Law 5: Know when and if you should invest in the "unknown."

Unknown investments are secondary investments. This type of investment can fluctuate. It may go up or down. Examples of unknown investments would be stocks, bonds, securities, market trades, or business ventures. There is always some risk involved in these types of investments. Do not use money dedicated to your known investments for unknown investments. Money for unknown investments can be put in your budget when you have extra money and have met all of your basic known responsibilities. Remember, before you start investing in several unknown investments, make sure you have paid off a considerable amount or all of your outstanding debt. We want to make getting out of debt one of our priorities. As we follow God's principles, our financial affairs and circumstances should be changing and getting better and in order. Step-by-step, we should be increasing and getting out of debt. Eventually we should have more than enough to sow into the kingdom of God, to invest in the needs of others, to invest in charities, and to sow into personal unknown investments for ourselves.

When you are ready and can afford to move into these types of unknown investments (which are unsure and possibly risky), get good, sound advice so that the money you put into them will bring the highest yield and profits. It is a good idea to consult with a financial advisor so they can help put your money to work for your benefit and profitability. If you have more, you can give more. God loves a cheerful giver. He wants us to do good works.

The key to any investment is timing—knowing when and when not to invest. Use good, godly wisdom in everything that you do. Be led by the Word and the Spirit of God. Ecclesiastes 3:1 says, "To every thing there is a season, and a time to every purpose under the heaven."

Law 6: Build the confidence to have what it takes to grow your money and your life.

It takes courage to build your finances and reach financial freedom. Without faith in God, we will never get the kind of courage and confidence we need to get to our goal. Without our connection with God, we will never get the kind of increase that we need and desire in our lives. It takes courage to increase and to be wealthy. You cannot be concerned with what others think about your ability to increase in God. You have to determine that you will go to the next level with God, no matter who tries to stop you or pull you down.

Success is available to anyone and everyone who will follow His ways. This is because God is not a respecter of persons. Acts 10:34–35 says, "Then Peter opened his mouth, and said, Of a truth I perceive that God is no respecter of persons: but in every nation he that feareth him, and worketh righteousness, is accepted with him." If we will follow the will of God and the plan of God, each of us will have our own measure of success in our lives.

God commissioned Joshua to take the place of Moses, lead the people, go over the Jordan, and finish the journey into the Promised Land He gave to them (Josh. 1:1–4). Obviously, this was not going to be an easy task. In verse 7, the Lord spoke to Joshua, saying, "Only be strong and very courageous, that you may observe to do according to all the law which Moses My servant commanded you; do not turn from it to the right hand or to the left, that you may prosper wherever you go" (NKJV). As long as Joshua followed what God instructed him to do, he was promised success. He had to be strong and courageous.

In the same way, it will not be an easy journey on the road to building your wealth. There will be many obstacles and roadblocks to overcome. Don't let them hinder your progress. You are going to have to be confident in who you are and maintain that confidence throughout the process. Don't pay attention to the negative things people will say or the negative feedback. Focus on your financial goals, develop discipline, and be diligent. Surround yourself with positive people who can give you good, godly wisdom and advice. Follow God and His Word, and you will prosper and have good success, just as Joshua did.

Law 7: Be thankful and grateful to God and remember that He gives the increase.

One of the things we are instructed to do in regard to holy living is found in 1 Thessalonians 5:18, which says, "In everything give thanks; for this is the will of God in Christ Jesus for you" (NKJV). *We should always be thankful to God, in all things and at all times.* As we learned earlier in Deuteronomy 8:18, God is the one who gives us the power to get wealth. As we honor God continually with our thanksgiving and our gratefulness, He will continue to bless us as we follow Him and the principles that He gives us in His Word. As we move forward, one day at a time, in building wealth, we have to remember that our victory in this area comes from our obedience to do it His way. We go out and do the work, but we have to remember that we must build a solid foundation by using and following the principles and precepts of God.

The Bible says this in 1 Corinthians 3:5–7: "Who then is Paul, and who is Apollos, but ministers through whom you believed, as the Lord gave to each one? I planted, Apollos watered, but God gave the increase. So then neither he who plants is anything, nor he who waters, but God who gives the increase" (NKJV). One of the reasons we have to be so grateful and thankful to God is because He is the one who is responsible for every increase and every blessing we receive. On your journey to financial freedom, every step of the way, remember to be thankful and grateful to Him. Keep your focus and your eyes on God because He is your source.

God is such a good God. Psalm 103:1–5 says, "Bless the LORD, O my soul; and all that is within me, bless His holy name! Bless the LORD, O my soul, and forget not all His benefits: who forgives all your iniquities, who heals all your diseases, who redeems your life from destruction, who crowns you with lovingkindness and tender mercies, who satisfies your mouth with good things, so that your youth is renewed like the eagle's" (NKJV). God wants to give us good things in life. Therefore, we must not forget to be thankful and grateful. We must honor Him, and rightfully so. He desires for you to have financial increase. He wants you to have financial success and obtain financial independence. Moreover, He wants you to have financial freedom.

Chapter Three

THE TRUST FACTOR

IIIIIIIIIIIIIIIIIIIIIIIIIIIIIIIIIIII

C AN YOU, WILL you, do you trust God with your money? Let us begin this chapter by looking at one of the scenarios in the Bible concerning the young rich ruler. This is what took place:

> And when he was gone forth into the way, there came one running, and kneeled to him, and asked him, Good Master, what shall I do that I may inherit eternal life? And Jesus said unto him, Why callest thou me good? there is none good but one, that is, God. Thou knowest the commandments, Do not commit adultery, Do not kill, Do not steal, Do not bear false witness, Defraud not, Honour thy father and mother. And he answered and said unto

him, Master, all these have I observed from my youth. Then Jesus beholding him loved him, and said unto him, One thing thou lackest: go thy way, sell whatsoever thou hast, and give to the poor, and thou shalt have treasure in heaven: and come, take up the cross, and follow me. And he was sad at that saying, and went away grieved: for he had great possessions. And Jesus looked round about, and saith unto his disciples, How hardly shall they that have riches enter into the kingdom of God! And the disciples were astonished at his words. But Jesus answereth again, and saith unto them, Children, how hard it is for them that trust in riches to enter into the kingdom of God! It is easier for a camel to go through the eye of a needle, than for a rich man to enter the kingdom of God. And they were astonished out of measure, saying among themselves, Who then can be saved? And Jesus looking upon them saith, With men it is impossible, but not with God: for with God all things are possible. Then Peter began to say unto him, Lo we have left all, and have followed thee. And Jesus answered and said, Verily I say unto you. There is no man that hath left house, or brethren, or sisters, or father, or mother, or wife, or children, or lands, for my sake, and the gospel's, but he shall receive an hundredfold now in this time, houses, and brethren, and sisters, and mothers, and children, and lands, with persecutions; and in the world to come eternal life.

—MARK 10:17–30

Obviously, the young rich ruler was not one who really trusted God. He loved his money and possessions more than he loved God. His faith and trust were in the things that he had and not God. He was sad and found it difficult to release his goods, sell his possessions, and get rid of his things in order to follow Jesus and be saved. His confidence was not in the one who could save him.

Confidence and trust in God is very important when you are following His plan and doing things God's way. If you are going to follow godly principles as a means to your goal to accomplish financial freedom, then you should trust God, who is the author of those principles—principles He established in His Word. When you embark on a journey or set your sights on a goal, you have to do it wholeheartedly. In other words, you want to do it unreservedly, enthusiastically, passionately, with all your heart. You want to devote yourself to accomplishing that goal. Your trust in the God who is helping you to accomplish that goal should be the same.

A few synonyms for the word *trust* are as follows: faith, belief, hope, confidence, expectation, and dependence. Therefore, if we trust God, we should have faith in God. Hebrews 11:6 says, "But without faith it is impossible to please him: for he that cometh to God must believe that he is, and that he is a rewarder of them that diligently seek him." I want to go a little further and examine one more translation of Hebrews 11:6 so that you can get a full understanding. The Amplified Version says this: "But without faith it is impossible to please and be satisfactory to Him. For whoever would come near to God must [necessarily] believe that God exists and that He is the rewarder of those who earnestly and diligently seek Him [out]."

We need to know the mechanics of our faith so that it will work for us. Our faith ought not be presumptuous. It needs to be appropriate or suitable to the will and the Word of God. There is a proper balance in everything that God does, and if we don't learn that balance, we can miss the mark that we are seeking very easily. It could appear that we are misusing our faith. If we do not have faith or trust in God, we cannot please Him.

Let's look at some areas in the Scripture that talk about pleasing God. Proverbs 16:7 says, "When a man's ways please the LORD, he maketh even his enemies to be at peace with him." What's the difference between your ways and your faith? Your faith helps you produce the kind of ways that are acceptable to God. As a Christian, if you have contrary or derogatory ways, if you are always bitter, upset, angry, negative, and outside the purpose God has called you to, most of the time your faith is not going to develop. This is because there are negative forces keeping you in a place of prolongation in these ungodly ways and not letting you get into the area of faith that you need to be in. It is always better to be an optimistic Christian and not a pessimistic Christian.

People who have their faith developed never have to worry about detours or being shipwrecked. This is why you must trust and have faith in God. There will be times in the process of developing your wealth that obstacles and detours will come, but as long as you have faith in God and His Word, things will get back on course. You can work your faith—that is, exercise, or better yet, use your faith—as long as your beliefs are aligned with the Word of God. We must always listen and follow what the Word of God instructs us to do. This is considered being wise. A wise person always listens to good instructions. You must always allow your ways to please God.

Let's review two more scriptures that talk about our confidence in God and pleasing Him. First John 3:21–22 says, "Beloved, if our heart condemn us not, then have we confidence toward God. And whatsoever we ask, we receive of him, because we keep his commandments, and do those things that are pleasing in His sight." When we keep His commandments and do the things that are pleasing to Him, God is ready to grant what we ask. Your faith in Him must always be strong, sincere, fervent, passionate, and full of wholeheartedness, as I pointed out earlier. We should have no fear or doubt to trust God concerning our money. We must follow *His* financial principles and precepts, and then we will receive from Him in whom we put our trust. When we obey and follow the will of God, we please Him. Sometimes you may have to deny your will, wants, and desires to please Him. This is not always easy. Some things that are required of us by the will of God may seem very hard at the time, but in the end, our faithfulness will bring significant victory.

Even Christ had to submit to the will of God when He felt it was too difficult for Him at the time. We see His submission to God's will in Gethsemane in the following scenario:

> Coming out, He went to the Mount of Olives, as He was accustomed, and His disciples also followed Him. When He came to the place, He said to them, "Pray that you may not enter into temptation."
>
> And He was withdrawn from them about a stone's throw, and He knelt down and prayed, saying, "Father, if it is Your will, take this cup away from Me; nevertheless *not My will, but Yours, be done.*"
> —LUKE 22:39-42, NKJV,
> EMPHASIS ADDED

Christ wanted the responsibility of the cup removed from Him. He did not want to go through the sufferings that His crucifixion would bring. Nevertheless, He submitted to the will of the Father, and a great victory was won. His victory brought redemption and salvation to all who will receive through faith in Him, Christ Jesus. *What a great triumph!*

Something I observed and find interesting and amazing is found in the next verse. Luke 22:43 says, "Then an angel appeared to Him from heaven, strengthening Him" (NKJV). As soon as Jesus submitted to the will of God, He got help. Angels came and strengthened Him. What I observed in that situation is that as soon as you let your will be God's will, help is on the way! If you keep your attitude right and have a heart and mind to please God, the challenges you face cannot stay.

The right attitude and the right motives are key players in having a heart to please and trust God. Philippians 4:5–8 (NKJV) says this:

> Let your gentleness be known to all men. The Lord is at hand.
>
> Be anxious for nothing, but in everything by prayer and supplication, with thanksgiving, let your requests be made known to God; and the peace of God, which surpasses all understanding, will guard your hearts and minds through Christ Jesus.
>
> Finally, brethren, whatever things are true, whatever things are noble, whatever things are just, whatever things are

pure, whatever things are lovely, whatever things are of good report, if there is
any virtue and if there is anything praise-
worthy—meditate on these things.

You need to let your lifestyle, your thinking pattern, and your attitude be as described in the afore-
mentioned scripture verses from Philippians. When the
opportunity knocks, our minds should be on the things
listed in verse 8. We always want to please God. You are
a complex individual who is able to discern and com-
partmentalize your thinking. Being able to manage and
organize your thought patterns in this way will help
you to be successful as a child of God.

Always remember you have to come to God with
the right attitude. The perfect time to build up your
spirit man through faith in the Word of God is when
things are going smoothly in your life. This way, when
an obstacle or a crisis comes, you can go straight to
God, quote His Word to Him, and trust that He is able
to perform His promises.

Abraham had this kind of faith. Romans 4:19–21,
says, "And not being weak in faith, he did not consider
his own body, already dead (since he was about a hundred years old), and the deadness of Sarah's womb. He
did not waver at the promise of God through unbelief,
but was strengthened in faith, giving glory to God, and
being fully convinced that *what He had promised He
was also able to perform*" (NKJV, emphasis added).

We please God when we have the right motives.

Have an attitude of faith. Have an attitude of trust. Don't waver in your belief in God and His Word. Keep the Spirit of God at the forefront, and let the Holy Spirit guide you in your motives in all that you do. Do not "half step" in life. Take full, bold steps, knowing in whom you trust.

Another area we reviewed relevant to having faith and trust in God, referring back to Hebrews 11:6, is that you have to believe that God is—that He exists. Consider Colossians 1:15–17, which says, "[Now] He is the exact likeness of the unseen God [the visible representation of the invisible]; He is the Firstborn of all creation. For it was in Him that all things were created, in heaven and on earth, things seen and things unseen, whether thrones, dominions, rulers, or authorities; all things were created and exist through Him [by His service, intervention] and in and for Him. And He Himself existed before all things, and in Him all things consist (cohere, are held together)" (AMP). For further scripture reference, see Proverbs 8:22–31.

The Scriptures clearly tell us that God exists. Not only does the Word tell us that God exists, but John 1:1–2 says, "In the beginning was the Word, and the Word was with God, and the Word was God. He was in the beginning with God" (NKJV). In the same chapter, in verse 14, it says, "And the Word became flesh and dwelt among us, and we beheld His glory, the glory as of the only begotten of the Father, full of grace and truth" (NKJV). How much more evidence do we need?

Look around you; look in the mirror and you will see His creations (see Genesis 1:1–31; 2:1–25, NKJV).

Read the Bible regularly and study the Word daily. This will build your faith in God and His existence. Romans 10:17 says, "So then faith cometh by hearing, and hearing by the word of God." When we operate in faith, we should not only believe that God is, but as Christians, we must also believe that He is the supreme and ultimate God in our lives. Exodus 20:3 says, "Thou shalt have no other gods before me." This means that Buddha can't be your god, money can't be your god, your education can't be your god, and material things cannot be your god. As you seek financial success, always put your trust in the true and living God. First Timothy 6:17 says, "Command those who are rich in this present age not to be haughty, nor to trust in uncertain riches but in the living God, who gives us richly all things to enjoy" (NKJV). Read and reflect on 1 Thessalonians 1:9 and Jeremiah 10:10–16.

After you have settled in your heart the fact that God is, that He does exist, and you trust Him and have faith in His Word, then you can believe the latter part of Hebrews 11:6, which says, "He is a rewarder of them that diligently seek Him." Having the faith you need to please God, and trusting Him as well, then the next step is believing that He will reward you when you seek Him. That is, when you look for, search for, hunt for, try to find and seek Him out and His way of living and doing things, then you should expect your reward.

Proverbs 11:18 says, "The wicked man does deceptive work, but he who sows righteousness will have a sure reward" (NKJV). If you follow, perform, and carry out God's right way of doing things, then your reward will come—even in the area of your finances.

Follow God's principles. Handle your financial business correctly. Make sure everything is done decently and in order. Diligence is not always easy. It takes a lot of hard work; it takes practice, patience, endurance, and stamina. Diligence requires *staying power.* Staying power requires lots of determination and perseverance. When it gets a little tough, the tough get going—you cannot give up.

I remember when I received the Lord as my Savior, I knew I was going to move ahead, and I was not going to be in the same condition two years later. I had the desire to grow. I remember telling the Lord, "Lord, I'm living by Your Word; I'm trusting Your Word. You healed my body; You touched my life, and You gave me a great jumpstart, and I intend to grow."

I would get up faithfully every day at three o'clock in the morning to study the Word. I read every book that my Bible school chancellor, Dr. Lester Sumrall, wrote. I would read his books constantly. I had only met him one time in my life, but I had the desire to seek God and grow. I could not even go to the campus or live on campus, because I could not afford to go away to school and still support my family. I remember that I wanted everything God had for my life. I would get up at three o'clock in the morning and take the exams for the correspondence school courses.

The money came to pay for the books, to pay for the courses, to pay for the videos, to pay for the literature, and to pay for the equipment. Every dime came in to pay for everything. I don't even know how God did it! All I know is that the money came. I do not know how in the world I did it financially, but I knew it was God. I continued in that way for years until I graduated and received my diploma, studying the Word of God.

If you are diligent and faithful, God will meet your needs, too. He will bring to you what you need. He will direct you and reward you.

Then I said to God, "Two years from now, Lord, I do not want to be in the same predicament and in the same place. I would like to own a house. I'm tired of staying in this apartment, and I want a home for my family." I was in school one day, standing in line, and I was holding some school grant papers in my hand. I was getting ready to register for full-time status at Florida Memorial College to finish my bachelor's degree.

Right then, I heard the Lord say to me, "Would you like to have a job?" I answered, "Yes I would." Well, guess what—I got a job! In addition, it was a job that paid quite a bit of money. The job also had requirements and criteria that I was not qualified for or skilled for. The math requirements included knowing Algebra II, a subject in which I was not proficient. I prayed and asked God to help me. I said, "God, if You help me, I know I will pass the algebra section on the test." Knowing that I had to do the algebra was frightening; nevertheless, I refreshed my knowledge on the subject, and I took the test and passed!

All of a sudden, on the day of my interview, I got terribly sick, and I did not know what was happening to my body. I went home, lay down, prayed, and went back full force the next day with enthusiasm. I interviewed, and was hired for the job. I knew I needed to seek the Lord for favor because I wanted to make permanent, full-time employment in one month. Many people had been there on the job for more than a year and had not been promoted to full-time employment. I fasted and prayed for twenty-four hours. I continued on the job and excelled to permanent, full-time employment within one month. You see, God will meet you where you are. Then I moved on to another department, became the leading supervisor, and was awarded a bonus every month.

When you diligently seek the Lord, He will reward you and meet your needs. When you do things decently and in order and make it a priority to please God and follow His ways, He will reward you. Trusting God—having faith in Him—is a key factor in having financial success and achieving financial freedom.

Let's take time to review a biblical character who trusted God. Hebrews 11:7 says, "[Prompted] by faith Noah, being forewarned by God concerning events which as yet there was no visible sign, took heed and *diligently* and *reverently* constructed and prepared an ark for the deliverance of his own family. By this [his faith which relied on God] he passed judgment and sentence on the world's unbelief and became an heir and possessor of righteousness (that relation of being right into which God puts the person who has faith)" (AMP, emphasis added). If we take a look at Genesis 5:32, it says, "And Noah was five hundred years old: and Noah begat Shem, Ham, and Japheth." In this scripture, the Bible describes Noah as being five hundred years old. Let's look at another scripture to make a point that I observed. Genesis 7:6 says, "And Noah was six hundred years old when the flood of waters was upon the earth." This specifies that a period of one hundred years passed between the time Noah was instructed to build the ark and when the flood actually came. Genesis 7:11–18 says:

> In the six hundredth year of Noah's life, in the second month, the seventeenth day of the month, the same day were all the fountains of the great deep broken up, and the windows of heaven were opened. And the rain was upon the earth forty days and forty nights. In the self-same day entered Noah, and Shem, and Ham, and Japheth, the sons of Noah, and Noah's wife, and the three wives of his sons with them, into the ark; they, and every beast after his kind, and all the cattle after their kind, and every creeping

> thing that creepeth upon the earth after
> his kind, and every fowl after his kind,
> every bird of every sort. And they went
> in unto Noah into the ark, two and two
> of all flesh, wherein is the breath of life.
> And they that went in, went in male
> and female of all flesh, as God had com-
> manded him: and the LORD shut him in.
> And the flood was forty days upon the
> earth; and the waters increased, and bare
> up the ark, and it was lift up above the
> earth. And the waters prevailed, and were
> increased greatly upon the earth; and the
> ark went upon the face of the waters.

Notice that in this scripture text, the Lord shut the door to the ark. We can only imagine that there were probably hundreds upon hundreds and thousands upon thousands of people who knocked on the door of the ark continuously to get in, with no success.

The flesh man operates in the realm of "I'll believe it *when* I see it." The spirit man operates in the realm of "I'll believe it, and I *shall* see it." Faith operates in the realm of the spirit man trusting God. When you trust God and have faith in God, you will believe it before it manifests itself in the natural realm. That is how we operate in faith.

Hebrews 11:1 describes faith this way: "Now faith is the substance of things hoped for, the evidence of things not seen." That is what faith does. When you speak the

Word of God and say what God says and believe it in your spirit, your faith believes it shows up in the natural realm before it actually does. Therefore, those things that we have been hoping for, the things that God has promised us in His Word, become real or tangible to us in the earthly realm.

As you live your life in accordance with the Word of God, by faith, believing and trusting Him, you will move ahead gradually and progressively until you accomplish your goal, those things you hope for. Even in the area of our finances, God works the same. Noah trusted God; he was obedient to build the ark. In the end, he gained a great victory. He saved not only his life, but the life of his family as well. He had great confidence in God.

I can only imagine the number of people who ridiculed Noah about building the ark. On your journey to financial freedom, people may ridicule you about what you are doing. Do not get discouraged. Trust God, and keep His Word before you. Seek Him diligently. Learn the Word of God—meditate on it, ponder it, and think on it constantly. Zeal without knowledge is not good. *You have to feed your faith and starve your doubts as you pay your debts.* Believe it will happen, and take action. Faith without works is dead (James 2:17).

To make the journey to financial freedom a successful and godly life journey, you have to trust God, not only with your money but also in every area of your life. Proverbs 3:5–6 says, "Trust in the LORD with all thine heart; and lean not unto thine own understanding. In all thy ways acknowledge him, and he shall direct thy paths." God will direct your financial path if you let Him. Trust Him to give you creative ideas and inventions that will increase wealth in your life. Trust Him with your money. Let Him direct you to the right investment ventures. He is omniscient (all-knowing).

Finally, when trusting and having faith in God, remember Galatians 5:6, which says, "For in Jesus Christ neither circumcision availeth any thing, nor uncircumcision; but faith which worketh by love." The key and most important factor to a working faith is love. Faith cannot work without love. God is love, and we must operate by the love of God that is in our hearts (1 John 4:16). Proverbs 8:21 says, "That I may cause those who love me to inherit wealth, that I may fill their treasuries" (NKJV). God wants to bless us financially.

Love God, trust God, and have faith in Him. He will take you to your wealthy place.

Chapter Four

SEED FAITH, TIME, AND THE HARVEST

IIIIIIIIIIIIIIIIIIIIIIIIIIIIIIIIII

W HEN WE START living in God's realm of financial increase, it is important to understand that much of what we do in the kingdom is based on *seed faith*—faith that is a result of the seeds that we sow. A verse that establishes this principle is found in Genesis. If we take a look at Genesis 8:22, it says, "While the earth remaineth, seedtime and harvest, and cold and heat, and summer and winter, and day and night shall not cease." There is always going to be seedtime and harvest. This plays a part in our lives. There will be times when we are going to sow seed; there is going to be a span of time after the seed is sown; and then we are going to reap a harvest. This is a promise from God. The promise is that if you sow seed and you are patient enough to wait for that seed to germinate, take root, and begin to produce after its own kind, there will be a harvest. Generally, people do not like to wait for the time that it takes the seed to germinate, take root, and begin to sprout above the ground.

If we observe the natural process of a seed coming to maturity, there are many stages taking place underground that are unseen before the seed sprouts above the ground. Because we cannot see what is going on underground, we think that there is nothing happening. However, as we have confidence and trust in God, we are assured that according to the principle above, there is going to be a harvest. Now, we have to trust God and have confidence as we wait patiently to see the harvest. But it is sure that if we do not sow seed, we can't expect to see a harvest.

We are talking about a dynamic principle in the Word of God. A principle works no matter who is following it or working it. God's principles do not change. Psalm 105:8 states, "He hath remembered his covenant for ever, the word which he commanded to a thousand generations." God remembers what He promises and what has been written in His Word. Therefore, the principles in His Word do not change. Once God says it, it does not change. This is one of the reasons why we can have so much faith and confidence in Him and His Word. Deuteronomy 7:9 states, "Know therefore that the LORD thy God, he is God, the faithful God, which keepeth covenant and mercy with them that love him and keep his commandments to a thousand generations."

God's principles work relational to relational, all things being equal. They do not pertain only to a farmer sowing seed for a food harvest. Galatians 6:7–8 states, "Be not deceived; God is not mocked: for whatsoever a man soweth, that shall he also reap. For he that soweth to his flesh shall of the flesh reap corruption; but he that soweth to the Spirit shall of the Spirit reap life everlasting." Even Job realized this, for Job 4:8 says, "Even as I have seen, they that plow iniquity, and sow wickedness, reap the same."

For example, let's say that you wanted more friends or you needed love and understanding. If you began to sow seeds of love, friendliness, or understanding and you were patient to see the results/reproduction of those types of seed sown, then that is the harvest you would receive. You would receive love, you would receive understanding, and you would receive friends.

If you sow apple seed, you will get apples. If you sow seeds of obedience, you will reap obedience. If a farmer never goes out to sow corn seed, there is no way the farmer would receive a harvest of corn during harvest time. He would not even go out and look for a harvest of corn, because he would know he had never sown corn seed.

It is the same with you and me; if we do not sow

seed, there will not be a harvest. We can pray, cry to God, whine, complain, and plead. We can do all of these things, but if we have not sown the right seed, we are not going to get a harvest. If you sow the right encouraging and constructive word seeds into your children, guess what? You are going to reap the right harvest. It doesn't matter if they look like they are batty, scatterbrained, or loony for ten years. This is your period of waiting—*your time.*

The Bible specifies seedtime and harvest. There is a waiting period before the harvest. This is the time that you have to be patient. During this period, it is very important to have patience. You have to believe that you sowed the seed and that the seed will produce. This is the promise of God. No matter how long it takes, if you believe and confess that you receive your harvest and hold fast to your confessions, you are going to reap the harvest of what you believe in and what you have sown. Hebrews 10:23 says, "Let us hold fast the confession of our hope without wavering, for He who promised is faithful" (NKJV). You have to have confidence. That confidence is in God's Word—it is not even in the seed at this stage. The confidence is in what God promised. God promised that if you sow it, you will reap it. You are going to get a harvest.

As we reviewed earlier in Genesis 8:22, while the earth remaineth—that is, for as long as time exits—there is going to be seedtime and harvest. Without a doubt, that principle is going to work, no matter what.

Without a doubt, it will work. So, hold fast to your confessions. Do not give up. Remain patient until you see your harvest manifest. Remember, God does not change His principles. He and his principles remain the same.

Let's look at another verse of scripture that contains a promise from God. Hebrews 6:13–15 says, "For when God made promise to Abraham, because he could swear by no greater, he sware by himself, saying, Surely blessing I will bless thee, and multiplying I will multiply thee. And so, after he had patiently endured, he obtained the promise." This scripture shows another example of the waiting period that takes place until your harvest manifests, or until what has been promised to you happens.

Remember, seed faith, time, and the harvest. It is important to remember to remain patient during this period. That is, wait patiently in faith with expectation. Psalm 27:14 states, "Wait on the LORD: be of good courage, and he shall strengthen thine heart: wait, I say, on the LORD." Even in this scripture, it emphasizes waiting. However, it tells us while we are waiting to have courage (guts, bravery, audacity, fearlessness). It also says that while we wait, God will strengthen us in our hearts, our spirit man. Even in our waiting, God is concerned about us. On the road to building your wealth, remember this. Have patience. It takes time to build wealth.

I want to review Galatians 6:9. It says this: "And let us not be weary in well doing: for in due season we shall reap, if we faint not." Here again is an example of the waiting time. Until due season, due time, we are patiently waiting and patiently enduring. Things are not going to happen overnight. But you have to patiently endure so that you can develop and establish your stamina to wait until you see the harvest. The Word of God says "in due season." Due season means *at the right time.*

We will reap if we faint not. If you do not give up, you will reap a harvest. That is the promise from God. If you do not faint, you will reap. Don't get tired. Don't give up. Don't throw in the towel. Don't lose heart. Don't be weary in doing what is right and what is the will of God, because in the right time, you will reap if you do not faint. If you are following the will and plan of God and sowing your seed and you have not received your harvest yet, that just means it is not time yet. You have to know in your heart that when it is time, it will happen.

For example, when it is time for a tree to bear fruit, the fruit will come forth, but if we take the fruit off the tree and pluck it before it is time (ripe for picking) and ready to eat, we will defeat the purpose of the fruit. We will lose the well-being or purpose of it.

You do not want to get ahead of God's timing. Many people do this and they shipwreck their lives. They shipwreck their families and they shipwreck their careers because they get ahead of God. They see what God is promising, and they see what God is doing, and they believe if God is showing it to them, then it ought to be for now. No, it may or may not be for now. *The promise of the harvest is for a due season.* It is for the right season and the right time.

In addition, I want to advise you not to compare your life to what you see someone else doing in his or her life. I say this because you do not know what kind of seed they have been sowing. You do not know how long they have been sowing their seed. You do not know how long it has been planted under the ground. And you do not know what has been going on with them and their affairs. Therefore, you cannot say, "They got their harvest, so I should have my harvest." No, you will get your harvest when it is *the right time for you.* You must trust God's timing. This means having confidence and trust in God. I talked about the trust factor in our previous chapter. As you study the Bible and trust God, the principles of His Word will be established in your heart. Then you will be able to take action in the areas of sowing and reaping in your life. This will help you to make good, sound, godly decisions when you begin choosing where and how to invest your income. Understanding God's system of sowing and reaping is a part of using godly sense to make dollars.

Matthew 17:20 talks about the topic of seed faith, which we have been discussing. It talks about sowing seeds of faith. Let's look at the scenario that leads up to Jesus' response in the above scripture. This is what took place:

And when they were come to the multitude, there came to him a certain man, kneeling down to him, and saying, Lord, have mercy on my son: for he is lunatick, and sore vexed: for ofttimes he falleth into the fire, and oft into the water. And I brought him to thy disciples, and they could not cure him. Then Jesus answered and said, O faithless and perverse generation, how long shall I be with you? how long shall I suffer you? bring him hither to me. And Jesus rebuked the devil; and he departed out of him: and the child was cured from that very hour. Then came the disciples to Jesus apart, and said, Why could not we cast him out? And Jesus said unto them, Because of your unbelief: for verily I say unto you, If ye have faith as a grain of mustard seed, ye shall say unto this mountain, Remove hence to yonder place; and it shall remove; and nothing shall be impossible unto you. Howbeit this kind goeth not out but by prayer and fasting.

—MATTHEW 17:14–21

In the above scenario, Jesus talks about having faith as a grain of mustard seed. Let's look at Mark 4:30–32, which says, "And he said, Whereunto shall we liken the kingdom of God? or with what comparison shall we compare it? It is like a grain of mustard seed, which, when it is sown in the earth, is less than all the seeds that be in the earth: but when it is sown, it groweth up, and becometh greater than all herbs, and shooteth out great branches; so that the fowls of the air may lodge under the shadow of it." Here, too, Jesus told the disciples they needed to have faith like a mustard seed. A grain of faith.

You may be thinking, "If only I had just a tiny little bit more of faith." If you look at a mustard seed, it is a very tiny little seed, one of the smallest seeds in the earth realm. However, the scripture states that when the mustard seed is sown, it groweth up and becometh greater than all herbs, and shooteth out great branches; so that the fowls of the air may lodge under the shadow of it. So then, what kind of faith is a grain of mustard seed? Jesus is not saying that you need just a tiny bit of faith. He is saying that if you have the smallest amount of faith, when you start sowing it, when you start working it and operating in it, it is going to sprout up and grow. It will not stay teeny-weeny. Your faith, the grain-of-mustard-seed faith, is the kind of faith that starts little but gets big. It does not stay little; it gets so big that it allows you to do great exploits. It sprouts up big. You have to "seed" your faith. You have to have seed faith. You have to have faith like a seed, which is not going to stay little but will sprout up big and grow strong. Your faith will grow strong.

If you are going to live effectively in the kingdom of God, you have to grow your faith. You have to exercise your faith. You have to build your faith, your confidence, and your trust in God. Because that's what faith is. Faith is confidence and trust in God and what God says. Faith is believing what God says in His Word. When you exercise your faith and it begins to grow, it will get so big that, as a result, people all around you will begin to glean from you and learn from you. Even the people around you won't stay in the little-faith mode. They will begin to follow suit and strengthen their faith as well. They will be encouraged by being around you.

Therefore, do not say that you have a little bit of faith. It may start out that way, as the measure of faith, but it will grow and become strong and great. *Have great faith.* As you believe God's Word, eventually your faith in God will get strong. When you have this kind of strong, great faith, it will remove doubt. When you have this kind of faith, you will have no problem with seeding into the things of God. You will have no problem with sowing. You will not fear sowing your seed.

Sometimes people fear giving. Sometimes people feel if they give, they will not have. This is contrary to God's principle. God's principle is that you give it, and you receive it. Luke 6:38 says, "Give, and it shall be given unto you; good measure, pressed down, and shaken together, and running over, shall men give into your bosom. For with the same measure that ye mete withal it shall be measured to you again." You cannot receive more seed from God if you hold on to all the seed you have. You have to open your hand and give it.

You have to have faith and confidence in God in order to release what is in your hand. If you keep your corn seed and do not sow it in the ground, will you receive a harvest? No. It is the same principle in relation to your finances. If you keep your ten dollars and do not sow it when the opportunity presents itself, you're not going to get a harvest from those ten dollars. So have great faith and sow your seed with faith and confidence in God and the principles of His Word.

Let's review the parable of the ten talents:

> "For the kingdom of heaven is like a man traveling to a far country, who called his own servants and delivered his goods to them. And to the one he gave five talents, to another two, and to another one, to each according to his own ability; and immediately he went on a journey. Then he who had received the five talents went and traded with them, and made another five talents. And likewise he who had received two gained two more also. But he who had received one went and dug in the ground, and hid his lord's money. After a long time the lord of those servants came and settled accounts with them.
>
> "So he who had received five talents came and brought five other talents, saying, 'Lord, you delivered to me five talents; look, I have gained five more talents besides them.' His lord said to him, 'Well

done, good and faithful servant; you were faithful over a few things, I will make you ruler over many things. Enter into the joy of your lord.' He also who had received two talents came and said, 'Lord you delivered to me two talents; look, I have gained two more talents besides them.' His lord said to him, 'Well done, good and faithful servant; you have been faithful over a few things, I will make you ruler over many things. Enter into the joy of your lord.'

"Then he who had received the one talent came and said, 'Lord, I knew you to be a hard man, reaping where you have not sown, and gathering where you have not scattered seed. And I was afraid, and went and hid your talent in the ground. Look, there you have what is yours.'

"But his lord answered and said to him, 'You wicked and lazy servant, you knew that I reap where I have not sown, and gather where I have not scattered seed. So you ought to have deposited my money with the bankers, and at my coming I would have received back my own with interest. Therefore take the talent from him, and give it to him who has ten talents.'"

—MATTHEW 25:14–28, NKJV

The servant with the one talent did not sow his one talent as the others did to reap a harvest. Instead, he held on to it and missed his opportunity to reap a harvest. In addition, the outcome of not sowing cost him the talent that he had. Do not be like him. Don't miss your opportunity to sow and reap. Don't miss your harvest. Do not let fear to sow keep you from your opportunity to increase.

Sowing, investing, and reaping are all a part of how we receive increase in our lives. We have to be willing to invest. You start with small investments and move into larger ones as you are in position to do so.

When we sow by investing, we should learn the language of investing. One of the first things to keep in the forefront when investing is: do not invest on a whim. Always do thorough research and gather good, pertinent information on the product you want to invest in before you invest. Use wisdom and be cautious.

One way to sow by investing is sowing and reaping through "unknown" investments. As we covered earlier, in chapter two under the fifth law of increase, unknown investments are secondary investments that can fluctuate, meaning they may go up or down. Unknown investments should be considered only when there is extra money readily available to you, money that is freed up (at liberty for you to use) in your budget (money management system).

There is always some type of risk involved in unknown investments. Unknown investments can offer income that is exempt from federal and/or state taxes, and some offer income that is taxable income as well. A few that offer income that is tax-exempt are municipal bonds, mutual bond funds, municipal preferred, tax-exempt money funds, and US government securities, which would include treasury bills, zero-coupon treasuries (STRIPS), and US government agency securities. On the other hand, a few that offer taxable income are certificates of deposit (CDs), commercial paper, corporate bonds, money-market funds, unit investment trust (UIT), and mortgage-backed securities, which would include Ginnie Maes, Fannie Maes, and Freddie Macs.

For more information on "unknown" investments, I would suggest reviewing the "Use IRA and Other Tax-Deferred Investments" section in chapter one, the "Minimize Risk by Diversifying" section in chapter one, the fifth law of increase in chapter two, and our *Financial Freedom Workbook*, which can be found under the "Other Books and Materials" section in the back of this book.

Your "unknown" investments will provide good options for diversification in your portfolio. A wise suggestion is, if possible, to have a good financial advisor. Financial advisors can help steer you in the right direction and help you to develop a financial portfolio suitable to your income and financial goals. As you begin to make your investments, always remember to have faith and trust in God. Your faith should not be in the product or the bond, but in God. *Faith in God produces the courage to be wealthy.* Prepare yourself to invest wisely and honestly. God wants you to increase. *Your seed faith will order your harvest.*

Remember to always invest in the "known" first. "Known" investments are our general living responsibilities and obligations. Make sure your family affairs and responsibilities are taken care of first. A reminder list of some of our basic known investments can be found in chapter one, again under the section titled "Use IRA and Other Tax-Deferred Investments."

Once you begin to get out of debt and stop overspending and overextending your budget, then you will begin to have extra dollars to invest in the unknown investments. The unknown investments bring in interest and dividends and allow us the opportunity to pay ourselves. These types of investments also allow our money to work for us.

When we have more money freed up to invest, it allows us another way to have seed money to sow in the form of investing. Second Corinthians 9:9–11 (AMP) says:

> As it is written, He [the benevolent person] scatters abroad; He gives to the poor; His deeds of justice and goodness and kindness and benevolence will go on and endure forever! And [God] Who provides seed for the sower and bread for eating will also provide and multiply your [resources for] sowing and increase the

fruits of your righteousness [which manifests itself in active goodness, kindness, and charity]. Thus you will be enriched in all things and in every way, so that you can be generous, and [your generosity as it is] administered by us will bring forth thanksgiving to God.

In these Scripture passages, we see that God gives us seed to sow. He gives us seed so we can eat, and He multiplies the seed that we sow. When you look at the option of sowing some of your seed through investing in unknown investments, it is multiplied back to you in the form of interests and dividends. One reason we should work toward getting rid of debt is that this process will make available to us extra, freed-up money to sow. Sowing it gives us the opportunity to multiply it. God multiplies the seed that we sow.

It is important not to sacrifice something you need. This should not be necessary if you are managing your money correctly and according to God's Word and His principles on finances. The scripture passage above tells us that God gives you some seed so you can eat. You should be able to take care of your family and take care of your needs.

According to these scriptures, you should have enough to sow, to give to your church, to give to charity, to give to the needs of other people, to sow into investments for yourself, and to take care of your home and your family. In addition, God will increase the fruits of your righteousness. This means God will bring it back to you again and cause your life to be such an example that there will be righteousness sown into the lives of other people—meaning, you will have more than enough to be generous and kind to others through charity and many other ways. God has it all worked out for us in this area! He has more than enough for us. God wants to bless us so that not only will we be blessed, but also so we can bless and be good to others.

You should never have to sacrifice the needs of your family to sow. God provides more than enough for us. This provision is clearly shown as follows: "And God is able to make all grace (every favor and earthly blessing) come to you in abundance, so that you may always and under all circumstances and whatever the need be self-sufficient [possessing enough to require no aid support and furnished in abundance for every good work and charitable donation]" (2 Cor. 9:8, AMP). You should never have to be sorrowful about not being able to give or sow when God has given you direction to do so. When you want to sow in an offering, sow into a good cause, or invest in a good cause or anything charitable, you should never feel sorrowful because you are not able to afford it due to financial lack. I say this because of 2 Corinthians 9:8. God says that we should always have enough to do the good works that He requires.

As children of God, we have to bring our financial situations in order so that we are always able to do what God has called and wants us to do. Many times we cannot do the things God wants us to do in these areas of good works because we are overwhelmed with debt. This can cause sorrow because we are not able to do what He asks. But remember, God does not want us to feel this way. God is El Shaddai. He wants us to have more than enough! He wants us to have what we need in abundance in order to do good works. He wants us to always, and under all circumstances, whatever the need, have sufficiency to do every good work.

We have to have confidence to sow seed. We have to have *seed faith*.

Here's another example to consider: In the natural realm, if you take a seed and sow it in the ground and reap the harvest, aren't you going to get back more by multiplication than the amount of seed you put in the ground? When the harvest comes up, it's going to be more than just the one or few seeds that you put in the ground. In the natural, you can see that. When you sow a seed, the harvest that comes back from that seed is multiplied.

If you sow an apple seed and wait the expected amount of time, a harvest should come forth during harvest time. Let's say harvest time is here and you go out, pick an apple off the tree, and cut it open. There will be more seeds in the one apple than you put in the ground, right? Right! The seeds in that one apple do not even take into account all the other apples with more seeds on all the trees in the rest of the orchard.

As children of God, we should not be afraid to sow

seed. Isaiah 55:10 says, "For as the rain and snow come down from the heavens, and return not there again, but water the earth and make it bring forth and sprout, that it may give seed to the sower and bread to the eater" (AMP). God will provide and give seed to the sower. And not only will He supply seed, but as we learned earlier, He will multiply the seed. He is such a wonderful, gracious, and kind God.

When you sow your seed, it will produce for you. Your increase from your seed will be multiplied. In addition, because it multiplies, you will have more seed to sow. You will have more seed to invest in your family, more seed to invest in the kingdom of God, and more seed to bless others so that the righteousness of God can be seen in your life. God loves it when we help others. We have to move forward in the things of God. We have to stay out of bad debt, debt that we accrue spending money on things that we do not really need and cannot really pay for. We have to get our financial affairs in order so that we can always be able to do the things that God wants and expects us to do. We must not give up until we reach financial freedom. We are following God's principles so that we can live a successful, godly life.

Since we have learned that God multiplies us in our sowing and increases us when we give, let's spend some time on our attitude toward giving. Since we have the love of God on the inside of us as Christians, we should always have a heart to give and to help others. We should make the effort to open our hands to give and partner with charities and nonprofit organizations to help aid their cause in helping others. You should give cheerfully and be happy and excited about your giving.

Second Corinthians 9:6–7 says, "But this I say, He which soweth sparingly shall reap also sparingly; and he which soweth bountifully shall reap also bountifully. Every man according as he purposeth in his heart, so let him give; not grudgingly, or of necessity: for God loveth a cheerful giver." In other words, if you sow in abundance, you will reap a great harvest. If you sow a little, you will reap a little harvest.

It all goes back to the heart. *Giving is a heart matter.* If you have a big heart to give, you will reap or receive in the same manner. Our attitude will take on the condition or state that our heart is in. If we have a big heart, full of love and ready to give, our attitude will reflect that.

Have you ever been given an assignment at home or at work that you did not really want to do? Nevertheless, you go in there and do it anyway, but with a bad attitude. It is the same with our attitude in giving. You have to *want* to give. You have to give because you love God. He is the source of all that we have. We will, and we must, be cheerful and excited in our giving. Think biblically, and do what the Word says you should do.

Proverbs 11:24 says, "There is that scattereth, and yet increaseth; and there is that withholdeth more than is meet, but it tendeth to poverty." You need to give what is necessary and remember you can't hold back more than you should. Let's look at Ecclesiastes 11:4–6, which says, "He that observeth the wind shall not sow; and he that regardeth the clouds shall not reap. As thou knowest not what is the way of the spirit, nor how the bones do grow in the womb of her that is with child: even so thou knowest not the works of God who maketh all. In the morning sow thy seed, and in the evening withhold not thine hand: for thou knowest not whether shall prosper, either this or that, or whether they both shall be alike good." If you are concerned about the circumstances in life rather than what God says, then you are not going to sow. If you don't sow, you are not going to reap. There is no way to reap a harvest if you do not sow. You can't pray in a harvest if you have not sown seed.

We are renewing our minds so that we are not afraid to give, to sow, or to invest. We can invest, give, and sow because that's the only way we are going to reap. If you don't put seed in the ground, you cannot expect a harvest. You have to sow seed. Genesis 26:12 says, "Then Isaac sowed in that land, and reaped in the same year a hundredfold; and the LORD blessed him" (NKJV). You have to release. Releasing and sowing show your freedom. It shows that you trust God to reap a harvest. It shows your confidence in God.

If we are going to experience financial freedom in our lives, we need to get free in the area of giving. You need to be in a financial position to sow your seed when the opportunities are presented because according to

Ecclesiastes 11:6, we do not know which will prosper. Remain faithful during your seed-growing time. Clear away financial clutter in your life. Take the opportunity to get rid of all unnecessary debt. *Put yourself in a position to sow and reap a bountiful harvest.* Don't miss the opportunity to allow God to multiply your seed.

On a final note, monetary giving is not the only way to sow, give, and invest. If you are not in a position to give monetarily yet, you can give of your time. Sow seeds from the heart. Do volunteer work as often as you can to help a good cause. Sow time into your local church and local charities. Sow your love to someone through a smile and friendliness. Let people see the love of God in you. As mentioned in other chapters of this book, God is love. He loves for us to give. Let someone see that the love of God lives in you. Look around you—there are many ways to sow the seed of love. Remember 2 Corinthians 9:8, which says God wants to supply you and furnish you in abundance for every good work and charitable donation. God is waiting to equip you to sow the seeds of love, faith, and finances.

Chapter Five

USING SENSE
TO
MAKE DOLLARS

||||||||||||||||||||||||||||||||||||||

EVERY DECISION WE make affects the quality of
the lives we live. In fact, the sum total of all the
decisions made and applied practically molds, shapes,
and influences the direction our lives take and where
we end up in this life journey. This is why the final three
chapters of this book are vital to the previous four. In
them, we will deal primarily with using the "sense" we
have to make dollars as well as the right choices.

What is "sense"? There are various meanings and
synonyms for the word. A few of them are intelligence,
brains, logic, intellect, common sense, good judgment,
and wisdom. I like the latter three best—and primarily

the last in the list, which is wisdom, because wisdom comes from God. He tells us in His Word to get wisdom. Let's review Proverbs 3:13–26 (NKJV) and see what the Word of God says about wisdom. These verses reveal the following about it:

> Happy is the man who finds wisdom, and the man who gains understanding; for her proceeds are better than the profits of silver, and her gain than fine gold. She is more precious than rubies, and all the things you may desire cannot compare with her. Length of days is in her right hand, in her left hand riches and honor. Her ways are ways of pleasantness, and all her paths are peace. She is a tree of life to those who take hold of her, and happy are all who retain her.
>
> The LORD by wisdom founded the earth; by understanding He established the heavens; by His knowledge the depths were broken up, and clouds drop down the dew.
>
> My son, let them not depart from your eyes—keep sound wisdom and discretion; so they will be life to your soul and grace to your neck. Then you will walk safely in your way, and your foot will not stumble. When you lie down, you will not be afraid; yes, you will lie down and your sleep will be sweet. Do not be afraid

of sudden terror, nor of trouble from the wicked when it comes; for the LORD will be your confidence, and will keep your foot from being caught.

Everything we have learned and covered in the four previous chapters will now come down to the sense or wisdom we use to apply to all areas of our lives that are applicable. At this point, that is what it is all about: *Using sense to make dollars.*

You have to use sense, what you have learned, to pursue the financial freedom you desire for your life. Third John 2:2 says, "Beloved, I pray that you may prosper in all things and be in health, just as your soul prospers" (NKJV). Your soul refers to your mind, your will, your intellect, and your emotions. How we perceive something in our mind and the way we think pertaining to a thing has a lot to do with our attitude about it. We have to have the thought pattern of the Word. Philippians 2:5 says, "Let this mind be in you which was also in Christ Jesus" (NKJV). We have to have the mind and the thought pattern of Christ (the Word of God).

Let's look at John 8:23–29 (NKJV):

> And He said to them, "You are from beneath; I am from above. You are of this world; I am not of this world. Therefore I said to you that you will die in your sins; for if you do not believe that I am He, you will die in your sins."

Then they said to Him, "Who are You?"

And Jesus said to them, "Just what I have been saying to you from the beginning. I have many things to say and to judge concerning you, but He who sent Me is true; and I speak to the world those things which I heard from Him."

They did not understand that He spoke to them of the Father.

Then Jesus said to them, "When you lift up the Son of Man, then you will know that I am He, and that I do nothing of Myself; but as My Father taught Me, I speak these things. And He who sent Me is with Me. The Father has not left Me alone, for I always do those things that please Him."

In the scriptures you just read, Jesus said, "When you lift up the Son of Man, then you will know that I am He, and that I do nothing of Myself; but as My Father taught Me, I speak these things." He also specifies that the Father has not left Him alone, for He always does the things that please the Father. Therefore, if we have the mind of Christ and the thought pattern of Christ, we have the mind and the thought pattern of God as well, because Jesus said He does nothing of Himself but as His Father taught Him.

Also, John 5:19–20 (NKJV) says:

Then Jesus answered and said to them.
"Most assuredly, I say to you, the Son can
do nothing of Himself, but what He sees
the Father do; for whatever He does, the
Son does also in like manner. For the
Father loves the Son, and shows Him all
things that He Himself does; and He will
show Him greater works than these, that
you may marvel."

Again, we see that Jesus does nothing of Himself but
only what He sees the Father do. That's confirmation!
He follows all things that the Father does. Having the
mind of Christ is a good thing. Consider this thought:
Who has more wisdom than God does?

If we study 1 Corinthians 2:11–16 (NKJV), it reveals
this:

For what man knows the things of a man
except the spirit of the man which is in
him? Even so no one knows the things
of God except the Spirit of God. Now we
have received, not the spirit of the world,
but the Spirit who is from God, that we
might know the things that have been
freely given to us by God.

These things we also speak, not in
words which man's wisdom teaches but
which the Holy Spirit teaches, comparing
spiritual things with spiritual. But the
natural man does not receive the things of

the Spirit of God, for they are foolishness to him; nor can he know them, because they are spiritually discerned. But he who is spiritual judges all things, yet he himself is rightly judged by no one. For "who has known the mind of the LORD that he may instruct Him?" But we have the mind of Christ.

According to Paul here, as Christians we have received the Spirit of God that we might know the things that have been freely given to us by God. It is so important to accept Christ as Savior and as the Lord of our life so that we receive salvation and have eternal life. By doing so, we also receive the Spirit of God through the Holy Spirit, who lives in us. Therefore, we can discern and know the things of God because His Spirit lives in us. There is absolutely no better way to live!

We have to use and apply the sense and wisdom of God in all areas of our lives. When we do this, we can prosper in all things as our soul (our mind, will, intellect, and emotions) prospers. The mind of Christ allows us to have access to the wisdom and knowledge of God.

God gives us revelation of His Word. The mind is the gateway to wisdom, knowledge, and understanding. It is the entrance, doorway, or way into everything we receive and perceive. When we begin to think like Christ our Savior, our actions will follow the direction of our thinking. Through the mind—the mind of the Spirit—we have an opportunity to think like our Savior.

We have to think with the mind of God in relation to our finances and everything we do. Thinking with the mind of God gives us the ability to accomplish things we never thought we could achieve.

When we follow the principles in God's Word that pertain to our finances, we are getting God's wisdom concerning that particular area or situation. We have the mind of Christ. As a result, we should always be thinking with the mind of Christ. Think God's Word.

Let's review a few more scriptures on wisdom and then we will move on. Proverbs 4:5–13 (NKJV) states:

> "Get wisdom! Get understanding! Do not forget, nor turn away from the words of my mouth. Do not forsake her, and she will preserve you; love her, and she will keep you. *Wisdom is the principal thing;* therefore get wisdom. And in all your getting, get understanding. Exalt her, and she will promote you; she will bring you honor, when you embrace her. She will place on your head an ornament of grace; a crown of glory she will deliver to you."
>
> Hear, my son, and receive my sayings, and the years of your life will be many. I have taught you in the way of wisdom; I have led you in right paths. When you walk, your steps will not be hindered, and when you run, you will not stumble. Take

firm hold of instruction, do not let go;
keep her, for she is your life.

—EMPHASIS ADDED

This exhorts that you must use the sense, the wisdom, of God on your quest to financial freedom. Wisdom is so important. According to the Word, it is the principal thing, meaning it is the chief, main, major, foremost, and most important thing. As Christians, we have the mind of Christ, and we have the Spirit of God, the Holy Spirit, living in us. This gives us personal access to God's wisdom. We must operate in it. The Word of God is godly wisdom.

Another aspect of using sense to make dollars is having the right attitude. As you learned earlier, how we think about a thing has a lot to do with how our attitude will be toward it. Attitude is all about mind-set. We discussed that we should be thinking with the mind of Christ. Wealth is not just about money. It is also about having the right attitude. I talked about creating a sense and an atmosphere of wealth all around you in earlier chapters, specifically in chapter one, "Twenty Steps to a Life of Financial Freedom."

You have to have an attitude or mind-set to hear from God and follow the instructions He gives in His Word. You have to have a mind-set ready to execute (perform) the instruction, trusting God, knowing and expecting His directions will bring good things. If you follow the instructions in His Word as it relates to your wealth and finances, you will not miss the mark you are aiming for.

You have to have the right attitude if you are going to accomplish the mission of gaining financial freedom. A part of that right attitude is knowing where the ability to get wealth comes from. Deuteronomy 8:18 says, "But thou shalt remember the LORD thy God: for it is he that giveth thee power to get wealth, that he may establish his covenant which he sware unto thy fathers, as it is this day." If we have the right attitude in knowing that it is God who empowers us to get wealth, then we will begin to operate with the mind of Christ and look for the streams of opportunities that He will put in our path.

What is a stream? A stream is a steady movement or flow of any liquid. In referring the stream to our financial situation, God will provide continuous opportunities for us to get wealth. We have to use the sense and wisdom He has given us to recognize the opportunities and know how to handle them in ways that will allow them to produce and flow like a stream for us, to move like liquid for us. That will allow our finances to overflow on our behalf like a gushing stream that overflows right over the riverbanks!

The next definition I want to mention is that of a fountain. A fountain is the source or beginning of a stream. If just for a moment, I want you to do a little bit of mental role-playing. I want you to imagine yourself as a fountain and remember that you are the beginning of a stream. You are a large fountain, and you make up many streams. There are many streams flowing from you. There are many gifts and talents that we have as individuals, which can work to our advantage to open up streams and doors of opportunities for us that will bring increase to our lives in a multitude of ways.

As we use the wisdom of God and operate with the mind of Christ, there will be many opportunities of financial increase, which will manifest through our God-given gifts (abilities and talents). Proverbs 8:11–12 says, "For wisdom is better than rubies; and all the things that may be desired are not to be compared to it. I wisdom dwell with prudence, and find out knowledge of witty inventions." Here we see again how important it is to have the wisdom of God. Wisdom allows us to tap into our various giftings for additional streams of increase—*using our sense to make dollars!*

Chapter Six

SENSE PAYS OFF

|||||||||||||||||||||||||||||||||||||||||

AS WE BEGIN to operate in the "God sense"—
wisdom that is God-given—many streams begin
to flow from our fountain. I want you to see an important story in the Bible about the life of someone whose
gifts, talents, abilities, and God-given wisdom provided
many streams of increase and income. His name is
Joseph. Joseph used his streams to their full capacity
and reaped a harvest of not only financial blessings, but
much more. He used his sense, wisdom, and abilities to
their maximum potential, and it paid off in dollars and
cents and much more. *Using sense pays off!*

I want to encourage you to read Genesis 37, 39, 40,
and 41 in their entirety to get full clarity and understanding of the story of Joseph. This will allow you to
relate fully to the points I will be making in the rest of

this chapter. I have inserted excerpts from the remarkable story of Joseph's journey from the pit to the palace. Familiarize yourself with it again as his incredible journey is revealed. Reflect on this astonishing passage and see how God-sense pays off. Follow the journey below:

> Now Jacob dwelt in the land where his father was a stranger, in the land of Canaan. This is the history of Jacob.
>
> Joseph, being seventeen years old, was feeding the flock with his brothers. And the lad was with the sons of Bilhah and the sons of Zilpah, his father's wives; and Joseph brought a bad report of them to his father.
>
> Now Israel loved Joseph more than all his children, because he was the son of his old age. Also he made him a tunic of many colors. But when his brothers saw that their father loved him more than all his brothers, they hated him and could not speak peaceably to him.
>
> Now Joseph dreamed a dream, and he told it to his brothers; and they hated him even more. So he said to them, "Please hear this dream which I have dreamed: There we were, binding sheaves in the field. Then behold, my sheaf arose and also stood upright; and indeed your

sheaves stood all around and bowed down to my sheaf."

And his brothers said to him, "Shall you indeed reign over us? Or shall you indeed have dominion over us?" So they hated him even more for his dreams and for his words.

Then he dreamed still another dream and told it to his brothers, and said, "Look, I have dreamed another dream. And this time, the sun, the moon, and the eleven stars bowed down to me."

So he told it to his father and his brothers; and his father rebuked him and said to him, "What is this dream that you have dreamed? Shall your mother and I and your brothers indeed come to bow down to the earth before you?" And his brothers envied him, but his father kept the matter in mind.

Then his brothers went to feed their father's flock in Shechem. And Israel said to Joseph, "Are not your brothers feeding the flock in Shechem? Come, I will send you to them."

So he said to him, "Here I am."

Then he said to him, "Please go and see if it is well with your brothers and well with the flocks, and bring back word to me." So he sent him out of the Valley of Hebron, and he went to Shechem.

Now a certain man found him, and there he was, wandering in the field. And the man asked him, saying, "What are you seeking?"

So he said, "I am seeking my brothers. Please tell me where they are feeding their flocks."

And the man said, "They have departed from here, for I heard them say, 'Let us go to Dothan.'" So Joseph went after his brothers and found them in Dothan.

Now when they saw him afar off, even before he came near them, they conspired against him to kill him. Then they said to one another, "Look, this dreamer is coming!"...

So it came to pass, when Joseph had come to his brothers, that they stripped Joseph of his tunic, the tunic of many colors that was on him. Then they took him and cast him into a pit. And the pit was empty; and there was no water in it....

Then Midianite traders passed by; so the brothers pulled Joseph up and lifted him out of the pit, and sold him to the Ishmaelites for twenty shekels of silver. And they took Joseph to Egypt....

Now the Midianites had sold him in

Egypt to Potiphar, an officer of Pharaoh and captain of the guard....

Now Joseph had been taken down to Egypt. And Potiphar, an officer of Pharaoh, captain of the guard, an Egyptian, bought him from the Ishmaelites who had taken him down there. The LORD was with Joseph, and he was a successful man; and he was in the house of his master the Egyptian. And his master saw that the LORD was with him and that the LORD made all he did to prosper in his hand. *So Joseph found favor in his sight*, and served him. Then he made him overseer of his house, and all that he had he put under his authority. So it was, from the time that he had made him overseer of his house and all that he had, that the LORD blessed the Egyptian's house for Joseph's sake; and the blessing of the LORD was on all that he had in the house and in the field. Thus he left all that he had in Joseph's hand, and he did not know what he had except for the bread which he ate.

Now Joseph was handsome in form and appearance.

And it came to pass after these things that his master's wife cast longing eyes on Joseph, and she said, "Lie with me."

But he refused and said to his master's wife, "Look, my master does not know what is with me in the house, and he has committed all that he has to my hand. There is no one greater in this house than I, nor has he kept back anything from me but you, because you are his wife. How then can I do this great wickedness, and sin against God?"

So it was, as she spoke to Joseph day by day, that he did not heed her, to lie with her or to be with her.

—GENESIS 37:1–19, 23–24, 28, 36; 39:1–10, NKJV, EMPHASIS ADDED

The story of Joseph's journey goes on and on. Eventually, Potiphar's wife accuses Joseph of sexual assault and Joseph is thrown in prison. Joseph gains favor with the keeper of the prison, who puts him in charge of all the prisoners. Later, Joseph is promoted by Pharaoh to be the overseer of all the land of Egypt because he interprets Pharaoh's dreams and is seen by Pharaoh as a wise and discerning man in whom is the Spirit of God (see Genesis 39:11–23; 40:1–23; 41:1–57, NKJV).

I wanted to share Joseph's journey because it shows over and over again how Joseph used his streams to reap a harvest of blessings in his life. By using sense and the wisdom of God, he was able to recognize his giftings and allow them to open up streams of opportunities that paid off and brought tremendous increase into his life.

Let's review some of the many ways that Joseph's

streams paid off as I recap some areas from the story passage of his journey.

When Joseph was sold to Potiphar, Potiphar observed that the Lord was with Joseph and made all that Joseph did to prosper. Because of this, Joseph gained favor with Potiphar, and he placed Joseph over all that he had. Potiphar made Joseph overseer of his house, and all that he put in his hand. This was a promotion from the pit, which his brothers threw him into, to being appointed overseer of Potiphar's house.

Later in the story, after Potiphar's wife accused Joseph of trying to sexually attack her, Potiphar threw Joseph in prison. However, even in prison, Joseph's stream of favor was operating, and God gave Joseph favor with the keeper of the prison—the keeper of the prison committed all the prisoners in the prison to Joseph's hand, and he became an overseer even there. The keeper of the prison did not follow up on anything Joseph did; he didn't look into anything that was under Joseph's command. That is what I call favor. The keeper of the prison knew that the Lord was with Joseph, and whatever he did the Lord made it prosper.

This reminds me of Psalm 1:3, which says, "And he shall be like a tree planted by the rivers of water, that bringeth forth his fruit in his season; his leaf also shall not wither; and whatsoever he doeth shall prosper." When we trust God and allow Him to direct our lives, even when it seems like it is a bad situation, He is there making sure everything works out right. Every situation that Joseph was put into, whether good or bad, everything he put his hand to prospered—even in a prison dungeon. Remember, no matter where you are, when God is with you, you will prosper.

There are many streams flowing through us that will bring forth increase. All we have to do is tap into them and use them. We all have gifts, talents, and abilities that God has endowed us to use. Joseph had an ability to interpret dreams, and when the opportunity arose, he used his gift to move forward. The gift made room for him, and doors of opportunity opened for him.

When Joseph was in prison, there were officers there who were previous servants of Pharaoh, the king. One officer in particular was Pharaoh's chief butler. He had a dream, but he was sad because there was no interpreter in the prison to interpret it. The chief butler told Joseph the dream, and Joseph interpreted it. Joseph instructed the butler that according to the interpretation of the dream, in three days Pharaoh would restore him to his position as chief butler. Surely, in three days Pharaoh had a birthday and made a feast for all his servants. He lifted the chief butler and restored him back to his post of butlership. The interpretation came to pass just as Joseph interpreted it.

In addition, Joseph had asked the chief butler to remember him when he was restored to his position with the king, but the chief butler did not remember Joseph. However, God does not forget us; this is why we have to trust Him. Man may forget, but God does not.

And then something happened two years later, as we saw in the story passage.

Two years passed by, and Pharaoh had a dream. You are probably thinking what I'm thinking. Opportunity arises again for Joseph to use his ability to interpret. His stream is flowing and is about to bring forth a great harvest.

When Pharaoh had his dreams, the next morning his spirit was troubled about the dreams, and he called for all the magicians and wise men. He told them the dreams he had dreamed, but none of them could interpret them. The chief butler observed this and told Pharaoh about the Hebrew, Joseph, who had interpreted his dream in prison. The chief butler also informed Pharaoh that his dream happened just as Joseph interpreted it. The dream came to pass.

After the chief butler shared his experience, Pharaoh called for Joseph. Can you imagine the path of Joseph's life at this point? Here was Joseph, thrown in the pit by his brothers, sold as a slave, become a servant, then an overseer, thrown into prison, then promoted to overseer of the prison, and now getting ready to appear before the king of Egypt! *When God's favor is on your life, good things can happen in the worst situations.* Promotion can take place in the midst of the impossible. Joseph's gifts, talents, and abilities were about to take him to a high level of promotion. His stream was still flowing. Joseph was not pushy, arrogant, or passing out business cards to exalt himself. No, Joseph was just flowing in the grace of God on his life.

So, Joseph was brought before Pharaoh, and Pharaoh told Joseph his dreams. However, before Pharaoh started revealing the dreams to Joseph, Joseph brought forth an important point. He stated, "It is not in me; God will give Pharaoh an answer of peace." Joseph acknowledged that his gifting to interpret dreams was not something that came from him but that it came from God.

Paul makes this point in 2 Corinthians 3:5: "Not that we are sufficient of ourselves to think any thing as of ourselves; but our sufficiency is of God." Even in Acts 3, when the man who had been lame from birth was healed and the people thought the healing came from Peter and John, Peter immediately responded this way: "Ye men of Israel, why marvel ye at this? or why look ye so earnestly on us, as though by our own power or holiness we had made this man to walk?" (v. 12; see also 4:8–10).

Joseph knew it was God's power in him to interpret the dreams. We saw earlier in the story that even Potiphar and the keeper of the prison knew God was with Joseph. The abilities and talents are in us. He is our Creator. Joseph knew his ability to interpret was from God, and he did not try to take credit for it. When we acknowledge God and put Him first, He is pleased with us. We learned earlier, in chapter one, about putting God first.

Now let's go to the next recap and see what Joseph did.

Joseph listened to Pharaoh's dreams and made the interpretation. He informed Pharaoh that his dream revealed there would be seven years of great plenty throughout all the land of Egypt, and after seven years of plenty would arise seven years of famine. He also informed Pharaoh that the seven years of famine would be very severe and deplete the land, and that the years of plenty would be forgotten. Now, at this point, another one of Joseph's streams kicks in—wisdom. His wisdom plays an important role as we continue to recap what occurred.

After the interpretation, Joseph gave Pharaoh a solution to the problem of famine that would arise. He suggested that Pharaoh select a discerning and wise man and put him over the land of Egypt, then appoint officers over the land to collect a fifth of the produce of the land of Egypt in the seven plentiful years. He then said Pharaoh should let the officers gather all the food of the good seven years and store up grain under the authority of Pharaoh and keep the stored-up food in the cities to use as a reserve for the land of Egypt during the seven years of famine so that the land of Egypt and the inhabitants would not perish.

Subsequent to Joseph giving his solution to Pharaoh, something amazing happens. Pharaoh thinks Joseph's advice is so good, he makes an amazing announcement and appointment. Because Pharaoh felt and believed

God had shown Joseph all that he had revealed and suggested, Pharaoh thought there was none as wise as Joseph—and he appointed Joseph over his house, gave him rulership over his people, and made him second-in-command to himself. *Wow—what an incredible promotion!*

Joseph used the wisdom, discernment, and gift of interpretation God gave him to open a great door of opportunity. He was a man who trusted God, remained diligent in his work, no matter what work environment he was put in, and kept allowing his streams to operate.

It makes sense to be in position to allow God to use you as He sees fit. Joseph did not let discouragement, where he was, what his title was, or any of the challenges he faced affect the spirit of God that was in him. This is truly a great example of God giving us the power to get wealth. God-sense pays off.

Now, let's move on; it gets even better. You are probably wondering, "Can it get any better than this?" Yes, it can!

More wonderful and great things happened that same day. Pharaoh also informed Joseph that he had set him over all the land of Egypt. Amazingly, Pharaoh took off his signet ring and put it on Joseph's hand. He also clothed Joseph in fine linen and put a gold chain around Joseph's neck. Then Pharaoh put Joseph in the second chariot to ride behind him, and they told the people of the land to "bow the knee" to Joseph. Can you imagine a country of foreign people bowing down to you? Absolutely incredible! It was almost as if Joseph was the king of Egypt himself.

Then Pharaoh made a remarkable statement. He said, "I am Pharaoh, and without your consent no man may lift his hand or foot in all the land of Egypt" (Gen. 41:44). Astonishing. Just truly incredible. How quickly Pharaoh turned over that much authority to Joseph! He didn't even take one day to go and think about it. When God is involved, it does not take His favor a long time to operate or go into effect. Joseph received immediate favor with Pharaoh. Suddenly, just like that, Joseph was set to rule over all the land.

Joseph used one of his streams. *He used the wisdom of God to give good advice to an important person.* We learned earlier in this chapter that wisdom is the principal thing. When we practice the principles of God and put action to the Word in our lives, it brings increase. God-sense, the wisdom of God operating in Joseph, gave him a solution to submit to Pharaoh concerning the famine. Wisdom, given to the right person at the right time, brought forth a tremendous blessing to Joseph.

As Scripture indicates, God gives us the power to get wealth. We have to use our God-sense, common sense, and good judgment—this God-given wisdom—to live the successful, godly life, a life full of abundance, increase, and the wisdom of God. You have to use this sense on your journey and passage into financial freedom. Use your God-given sense. Use a sound mind to make cents and to make dollars.

Joseph went out from the presence of Pharaoh that day and went throughout all the land of Egypt. Just as Joseph interpreted the dream, it came to pass. There were seven plentiful years, and the ground brought forth abundantly in the land of Egypt. Another harvest came forth as a result of Joseph using his gifts, talents, and abilities. Streams are flowing again. This is what happened.

As we just mentioned, the land did bring forth abundantly. In fact, the grain that came forth was so great in quantity that Joseph stopped counting it because it was so much. It was as the sand of the sea. Can you just imagine how much grain that would be? That is a lot of grain!

Joseph gathered up all the food of the seven years that was in the land of Egypt, as he had suggested to Pharaoh. He followed the plan he gave to Pharaoh and laid up the food in every city from the fields that surrounded those cities. Then, as Joseph interpreted, the seven years of plenty in the land of Egypt ended and the seven years of famine began to unfold. Famine was in every land, but in all the land of Egypt there was plenty of bread.

In fact, the famine was over all the face of the earth. Joseph's stream of wisdom is really going to pour in the increase because of what Joseph did next!

He opened all the storehouses and sold to the

Egyptians. But keep in mind, the famine was over all the lands of the earth. Therefore, no one else had grain but Egypt.

Moreover, who was in charge of this grain? Joseph! Joseph was the man to see. Are you thinking what I'm thinking? If your wisdom and common sense is operating similar to mine, then we have the same thought pattern, the thought pattern of thinking that all those other countries that were experiencing famine had to get their grain from somewhere. However, guess what? The only person with grain was Joseph, and Joseph was definitely in charge. As a result, Joseph now had the opportunity to sell grain to all the other countries because the famine was severe in all the lands—and that is exactly what he did! All countries came to Joseph to buy grain. What an extraordinary blessing—a blessing Joseph never would have expected to take place when he was inside the prison walls of Pharaoh. God can do the impossible, for with God nothing will be impossible (Luke 1:37).

Every one of those countries had to come and buy grain from Joseph. Can you imagine how much grain Joseph sold? Increase was coming in from the left and from the right. Increase came from the north, the south, the east, and the west. Joseph had used his sense, and it was bringing in the dollars! People from all over the country were lining up to buy grain from Joseph.

What you should observe and note from this story is that Joseph used the streams he had to bring increase into his life. He had favor, wisdom, the gift to interpret dreams, talents, and abilities. He used his sense to make dollars, and the sense paid off! Whether it was a promotion or wealth, it brought him into a state of financial freedom. Even before Joseph died at 110 years old, he had the opportunity to say this to his brothers: "But as for you, you meant evil against me; but God meant it for good, in order to bring it about as it is this day, to save many people alive" (Gen. 50:20, NKJV).

God not only blessed Joseph, but He allowed all the people who bought grain from Joseph to stay alive during the time of the famine. All the bad things and bad situations that Joseph experienced and found himself in brought about something good.

Joseph had many challenges, and he overcame them all. In each situation Joseph was put into, he prospered. He kept the right attitude no matter the situation. He trusted God, and God was with him. As mentioned in chapter five, God tells us in Scripture to get wisdom, as it is the principal thing.

Joseph used his God-given wisdom continuously. He used sense, and the sense paid off. Use the wisdom of God to advance you on your journey to financial freedom. It is free to all who ask for it, according to James 1:5. Take advantage of your giftings, and allow them to open streams of opportunities for you. Take a step of faith; your God-given wisdom is just a prayer away. *Use sense to make dollars!*

Chapter Seven

WISDOM
SPARKS
INNOVATION

||||||||||||||||||||||||||||||||||

T HE LAST THING that I want to talk about concerning our streams is the ability to be *innovative*. Innovation is so important. It has played a great part in making America the great country it is today, and it is still doing so. Innovation brought new ideas and inventions to America, which eventually brought on the great Industrial Revolution. The Industrial Revolution brought to America new industry, new jobs, and new prosperity. Innovation has played a great role even in how we spread the Good News (the gospel). Because of the innovative explosion in technology, we are now able to reach people not only in America with the gospel, but all over the world. Because of innovation in technology, we can spread the gospel through e-mails, downloads, podcasts, cell phones, computers, and much more.

A tiny innovative idea called the satellite started as a small innovative thought, became a huge phenomenon, and changed forever the way we communicate all over the world. Because of one innovative genius, Steve Jobs, who decided to put action to his innovative ideas and creativity in technology, we can now receive not only the gospel, but also a world of information through the iPod, iPhone, and iPad. Never underestimate the power of an idea, the power of wisdom, and its ability to deliver to us innovation (Prov. 8:11–12). Innovation is an important tool and a key player on the road to financial freedom. Keep wisdom close and your streams flowing. Take action on insight into new ideas as they come to you.

As we learned earlier in chapter five, Proverbs 8:11–12 says this: "For wisdom is better than rubies; and all the things that may be desired are not to be compared to it. I wisdom dwell with prudence, and *find out knowledge of witty inventions*" (emphasis added). The scripture states that wisdom dwells with prudence. Prudence means "to act with carefulness, discretion, and good sense." We saw in previous passages how Joseph approached Pharaoh with carefulness, discretion in what he said, and good sense in his responses, statements, and answers to Pharaoh. Think of being a representative of the president of the United States and going to another country to represent him. You would use good judgment, diplomacy, and tact when interacting with the leaders of that country. That is how I saw Joseph interacting with Pharaoh. Wisdom was dwelling in Joseph, and it took him into massive channels of increase.

What does it mean to be innovative? Some synonyms for the word *innovative* would be groundbreaking, pioneering, inventive, original, and new. When we have this wisdom, this God-given sense, operating in us, we have the ability to be innovative. As children of God, we should strive to be the first with new ideas, creations, inventions, and much more. The world is always interested in something new and fresh. They are just waiting for someone to give it to them or suggest it to them—just like Joseph's suggestion and advice to Pharaoh. Someone gave it to Pharaoh, and he thought it was good advice. It opened a great door of increase and opportunity for Joseph.

You might be saying, "Well, what are my skills, abilities, and talents?" They're there. You do have them. Just ask God to show you what they are. In addition, if you feel that you do not have any wisdom, you can ask. James 1:5 states, "If any of you lacks wisdom, let him ask of God, who gives to all liberally and without reproach, and it will be given to him" (NKJV). God gives His wisdom to us freely. It does not cost you anything.

Being innovative, being the pioneer of something,

always opens up doors of opportunity and gives you the chance to increase and move forward into financial freedom. Even in your work environment, you can be a pioneer. You may have ideas and suggestions that you think would be good for the company or that might bring increase, revenues, and profits to the company. Use prudence and share them with your boss or the proper personnel. You never know; they might like the idea or advice. It could be a stream that will flow abundantly for you.

God loves you; He desires good things for you. He wants to open doors of opportunity for you. He wants to give you the power to get wealth.

There is one other character in the Bible that I want to mention who knew the great importance of wisdom, and his name is Solomon. Solomon asked for wisdom, and God gave it to him and much more. Let's review the following scripture passage and see how important wisdom was to Solomon. This passage gives us an amazing look into an incredible Bible story about wisdom:

> Now Solomon the son of David was strengthened in his kingdom, and the LORD his God was with him and exalted him exceedingly.
>
> And Solomon spoke to all Israel, to the captains of thousands and of hundreds, to the judges, and to every leader in all Israel, the heads of the fathers' houses.

Then Solomon, and all the assembly with him, went to the high place that was at Gibeon; for the tabernacle of meeting with God was there, which Moses the servant of the LORD had made in the wilderness. But David had brought up the ark of God from Kirjath Jearim to the place David had prepared for it, for he had pitched a tent for it at Jerusalem. Now the bronze altar that Bezaleel the son of Uri, the son of Hur, had made, he put before the tabernacle of the LORD; Solomon and the congregation sought Him there. And Solomon went up there to the bronze altar before the LORD, which was at the tabernacle of meeting, and offered a thousand burnt offerings on it.

On that night God appeared to Solomon, and said to him, "Ask! What shall I give you?"

And Solomon said to God: "You have shown great mercy to David my father, and have made me king in his place. Now, O LORD God, let Your promise to David my father be established, for You have made me king over a people like the dust of the earth in multitude. Now give me wisdom and knowledge, that I may go out and come in before this people; for who can judge this great people of Yours?"

Then God said to Solomon: "Because

this was in your heart, and you have not asked riches or wealth or honor or the life of your enemies, nor have you asked long life—but have asked wisdom and knowledge for yourself, that you may judge My people over whom I have made you king—wisdom and knowledge are granted to you; and I will give you riches and wealth and honor, such as none of the kings have had who were before you, nor shall any after you have the like."

So Solomon came to Jerusalem from the high place that was at Gibeon, from before the tabernacle of meeting, and reigned over Israel. And Solomon gathered chariots and horsemen; he had one thousand four hundred chariots and twelve thousand horsemen, whom he stationed in the chariot cities and with the king in Jerusalem. Also the king made silver and gold as common in Jerusalem as stones, and he made cedars as abundant as the sycamores which are in the lowland. And Solomon had horses imported from Egypt and Keveh; the king's merchants bought them in Keveh at the current price. They also acquired and imported from Egypt a chariot for six hundred shekels of silver, and a horse for one hundred and fifty; thus, through their agents, they exported them to all the kings of the Hittites and the Kings of Syria.

—2 Chronicles 1:1–17, nkjv

Wow! Just think about it. If God Himself, the Creator of the universe and everything in it, told you to ask for whatever you desired, what would be your response? Probably many people would have asked for riches and wealth, but not Solomon. Solomon asked for wisdom. Having wisdom must have been very important to him. Solomon could have asked for anything that he wanted; God gave him an open invitation to ask for whatever he desired. Having wisdom, this God-given sense, was the number one thing that Solomon desired above all else.

Not only did God grant Solomon wisdom, but also He granted him wealth, riches, and honor. The wealth God gave to Solomon was more wealth and riches than any of the other kings had. Moreover, no other king after him in this era would have as much wealth and riches as he. The latter that Solomon received from God was another advantage and unexpected blessing. Solomon asked for wisdom, and he received it.

I also noticed in the scripture passage that we read concerning Solomon that like the Lord was with Joseph, He was with Solomon. In your quest to financial freedom, as I covered before in other chapters, trust God. Put Him first place in your life and all that you do. He will bless your life! Follow the principles in His Word, and they will teach you how to live a successful, godly life in an ungodly, immoral, and corrupt world. If you so desire, you can ask for the empowerment of wisdom to the same degree and measure that Solomon had. The Word of God tells us that God will give it (wisdom) to all who ask liberally (James 1:5). His Word will give you guiding principles and show you the pathway to success in every area of life.

If you don't know your abilities and you feel like you just do not know what to ask for, you can always ask for wisdom. As we saw in Proverbs, it is the principal thing. God will give wisdom to all who ask. When Solomon asked for wisdom, God gave it to him in such a large degree that Solomon became the principal author of the Book of Proverbs in the Bible. His wisdom and knowledge became so vast that he spoke 3,000 Proverbs and wrote 1,005 songs (see 1 Kings 4:32). God granted Solomon the wisdom he asked for and so much more. What a wonderful blessing God bestowed upon Solomon when He honored his request for wisdom!

Let's take a brief look into Solomon's life to see what a life filled with wisdom can bring. After God granted his request, we find Solomon reigning in life as follows:

> Judah and Israel were as numerous as the sand by the sea in multitude, eating and drinking and rejoicing. So Solomon reigned over all the kingdoms from the River to the land of the Philistines, as far as the border of Egypt. They brought tribute and served Solomon all the days of his life.

Now Solomon's provision for one day was thirty kors of fine flour, sixty kors of meal, ten fatted oxen, twenty oxen from the pastures, and one hundred sheep, besides deer, gazelles, roebucks, and fatted fowl.

For he had dominion over all the region on this side of the River from Tiphsah even to Gaza, namely over all the kings on this side of the River; and he had peace on every side all around him. And Judah and Israel dwelt safely, each man under his vine and his fig tree, from Dan as far as Beersheba, all the days of Solomon.

Solomon had forty thousand stalls of horses for his chariots, and twelve thousand horsemen. And these governors, each man in his month, provided food for King Solomon and for all who came to King Solomon's table. There was no lack in their supply. They also brought barley and straw to the proper place, for the horses and steeds, each man according to his charge.

And God gave Solomon wisdom and exceedingly great understanding, and largeness of heart like the sand on the seashore. *Thus Solomon's wisdom excelled the wisdom of all the men of the East and all the wisdom of Egypt.* For he was wiser than all men—than Ethan the Ezrahite, and Heman, Chalcol, and Darda, the sons of Mahol; and his fame was in all the surrounding nations. He spoke three thousand proverbs, and his songs were one thousand and five. Also he spoke of trees, from the cedar tree of Lebanon even to the hyssop that springs out of the wall; he spoke also of animals, of birds, of creeping things, and of fish. And men of all nations, from all the kings of the earth who had heard of his wisdom, came to hear the wisdom of Solomon

—1 KINGS 4:20–34, NKJV,
EMPHASIS ADDED

As you just read in the scripture passage above, it is absolutely incredible what God did for Solomon. A man who only asked for wisdom to rule the people of God rightly got so much more. When God is with you, there is no limit to what you can do! Not only did Solomon have wisdom, but also his wisdom excelled the wisdom of all the men of the East and all the wisdom of Egypt. Men from all nations who had heard of his wisdom came to hear the wisdom of Solomon. In Solomon's day and time, he was wiser than all other kings. As we saw in the passage above, there is no question about the amount of wealth that he had. Not only did he have wealth and riches beyond measure, but Solomon had peace along with his wealth. Many people have wealth with no peace. When God is with you, there is peace and wealth. Godly wisdom is important. Make sure that you ask for it. Read and study God's Word and His principles regularly. You will find wisdom in the Word of God.

I referred to Proverbs 8:12 earlier in the chapter, and it states that this wisdom gives us knowledge of witty inventions. I discussed the importance of being innovative and producing innovative ideas. I also covered how they can bring wealth and financial freedom to our lives. Travel on your road to financial freedom with vast ideas and creations in mind. Dare to be innovative! Dare to be a pioneer! Let the God-given wisdom inside you produce witty inventions, reveal new ideas, and catapult you into a stream of money-making ventures. Let your stream of creativity flow!

When you have the desire to want to do something or accomplish something that lines up with the will and the Word of God, just ask God, and He will impart wisdom. As we discussed earlier, God will give it (wisdom) freely to all who ask for it. As you desire to use your sense for good, God-given assignments and accomplishments, God will help you. That is exactly what He did with the children of Israel when Moses told them the instructions from the Lord—that they were to build the tabernacle and bring as an offering to the Lord whatever materials were needed to do the job. The key words in the passage are "whoever is of a willing heart" (Exod. 35:5, NKJV).

Let's review the following scripture passages and see what God did for those who had the desire and will to give, as well as the desire and will to use their skills (keep their streams of opportunity flowing). Reflect on these passages and see wisdom and innovation at work. This is what took place:

> And Moses spoke to all the congregation of the children of Israel, saying, "This is the thing which the LORD commanded, saying: 'Take from among you an offering to the LORD. Whoever is of a willing heart, let him bring it as an offering to the LORD: gold, silver, and bronze....All who are gifted artisans among you shall come and make all that the LORD has commanded.'"
>
> —EXODUS 35:4–5, 10, NKJV

So everyone whose heart was stirred, whose spirit was willing, and who had a willing heart came and brought an offering to the Lord to build the tabernacle, supply it, and fill it with everything that was needed for its services. Those who were willing brought gold, silver, bronze, jewelry, fine linen, animal hair and skins, acacia wood, and all that would be of use to build and supply the tabernacle (Exod. 35:21–25).

They came, men and women alike. Let's examine the following passages and observe what happened next when innovation was flowing because of God's wisdom:

And all the women *whose hearts stirred with wisdom* spun yarn of goats' hair. The rulers brought onyx stones, and the stones to be set in the ephod and in the breastplate, and spices and oil for the light, for the anointing oil, and for the sweet incense. The children of Israel brought a freewill offering to the LORD, all the men and women *whose hearts were willing* to bring material for all kinds of work which for the LORD, by the hand of Moses, had commanded to be done.

And Moses said to the children of Israel, "See, the LORD has called by name Bezaleel the son of Uri, the son of Hur, of the tribe of Judah and *He has filled him with the Spirit of God, in wisdom and understanding, in knowledge and all manner of workmanship, to design artistic works, to work in gold and silver and bronze, in cutting jewels for setting, in carving wood, and to work in all manner of artistic workmanship.*

"And He has put in his heart the ability to teach, in him and Aholiab the son of Ahisamach, of the tribe of Dan. *He has filled them with skill to do all manner of work of the engraver and the designer and the tapestry maker,* in blue, purple, and scarlet thread, and fine linen, *and of the weaver—those who do every work and those who design artistic works.*

"And *Bezaleel and Aholiab, and every gifted artisan in whom the Lord has put wisdom and understanding, to know how to do all manner of work for the service of the sanctuary,* shall do according to all that the LORD has commanded."

Then Moses called Bezaleel and Aholiab, and every gifted artisan in whose heart *the Lord* had *put wisdom,* everyone whose heart was stirred, to come and do the work. And they received from Moses all the offering which the children of Israel had brought for the work of the service of making the sanctuary. So they continued bringing to him free-will offerings every morning. Then all the craftsman who were doing all the work of the sanctuary came, each from the work he was doing, and they spoke to Moses, saying, "The people bring much more than enough for the service of the work which the LORD commanded us to do."

So Moses gave a commandment, and they caused it to be proclaimed throughout the camp, saying, "Let neither man nor woman do any more work for the offering of the sanctuary." And the people were restrained from bringing, for

the material they had was sufficient for all
the work to be done—indeed too much
—Exodus 35:26–36:7, nkjv,
emphasis added

As we see in the passages above, those whose hearts
were stirred, whose hearts were willing, and those who
had the desire to come and do the work, the Lord God
gave wisdom and understanding to know how to do all
manner of work for the service of the sanctuary. There
is no question that God will give you wisdom for what
you need to accomplish. God also filled them with
knowledge and skill to do all manner of workmanship.
God is so awesome! He filled them with the skill to
design and to do artistic work. He gave them the skill
and knowledge to become jewelers, tapestry makers,
designers, engravers, weavers, wood-carvers, experts
in gold, silver, and bronze, stone-setters, builders,
and much more. Talk about innovation and streams!
Streams were flowing at a maximum level.

As it has been said time and time again throughout
this book, all we need to do is trust God. In Him, we
can find whatever we need. Wisdom, knowledge, understanding, direction, information, intellect, talent, ability,
gifts—God our Creator has everything we need. All we
have to do is trust Him, have faith, and ask. He is a
rewarder of those who diligently seek Him.

There was an abundance of everything they needed.
Even the craftsmen and artisans asked Moses to tell
the people to stop giving because they had too much

of what they needed. Be willing and obedient to follow the will of the Lord. Be willing and obedient to follow His instructions. Be willing and obedient to follow the principles in His Word. Take the road to your financial freedom one day at a time, one step at a time. Seek God for wisdom. Discover what your various skills are. Discover what your gifts are. Use them to your best ability. Tap into every stream that flows for you. You are a large fountain with many streams coming from you. Trust God. *Use your sense to make dollars. Use your wisdom to be innovative.*

In addition, always make sure you gain as much knowledge and information as you can on income-producing streams, through resource-reading and research. A list of a few income-producing streams are as follows: income from a primary job or primary business, the tithe, seed-faith offerings, a part-time or second job, part-time business income, real-estate investments, annuities or insurance, charitable giving, investment counseling, savings account, stock market, trading investments, and creative income-making ventures. Always seek direction and consultation from an expert. Don't forget to do your research. Remember, your first expert is God, the one who created you.

On a final note, the last thing that I want to discuss concerning being innovative, using your streams, and taking advantage of your gifts, talents, and abilities is *being confident*. If we look at a few synonyms for the word *confident*, they describe being confident as being sure, being certain, being positive, being convinced, and being self-assured and in no doubt of one's self. As you travel on the road to financial freedom, be confident and positive about your God-given capabilities and talents.

As Christians, we can be confident in who we are, what we do, and what our capabilities are because we are made in the image and likeness of God, our Creator. Genesis 1:25–27 says, "And God made the beast of the earth after his kind, and cattle after their kind, and every thing that creepeth upon the earth after his kind: and God saw that it was good. And God said, Let us make man in our image, after our likeness: and let them have dominion over the fish of the sea, and over the fowl of the air, and over the cattle, and over all the earth, and over every creeping thing that creepeth upon the earth. So God created man in his own image, in the image of God created he him; male and female created he them." If we are made in the image of God and after His likeness, then we can be assured that there is creativity and capability in us. If the very Spirit of God, in this dispensation and time, now lives in us through the Holy Spirit, then His wisdom and creativity are in us.

If we take a glance around us and look at the earth and the environment we live in, we can see that God, our Creator, is full of creativity, wisdom, and innovation. If you step outside your door and just take a stroll or walk around the neighborhood, you can see His creativity. For instance, just by viewing the sky or the landscape, you can tell that He loves color, splendor, beauty, and diversity. If you study the plant system and how our crops grow, you can observe His wisdom, organization, timeliness, and order. If you were to study the composition, structure, and genetics of our human body, you would see and observe God's intelligence, astuteness, and vastness of knowledge. A quick study of the brain alone and its capabilities and functions reveals a super-wise and innovative God.

Therefore, if we are made in the same image and likeness as God, then we have all sorts of capabilities inside of us. We can be confident in who we are. We are like our Father, God. As Christians, we are His children. Even scientists will tell you that children take on similar traits of their father and mother. Being created in God's image and likeness allows us to have some of the same traits and character of our Father, God. As we follow the Word of God and renew our minds, our thinking becomes more like God's thinking.

As you go out on your quest and journey to financial freedom, be confident in who and whose you are. Know that there is creativity in you. Innovation and witty ideas are in you. Many streams will flow for you as you apply the God-given talent and giftings inside of you. God's wisdom is always inside of you. If you feel that His wisdom is missing, then according to His Word, all you need to do is ask. Just like the biblical characters Solomon and Joseph, God is with you. His very Spirit lives inside of you if you are a Christian.

Move out on your journey with confidence. Trust God, and know that He is always with you. *Use your sense to make dollars.* Be creative, be innovative, and be a pioneer.

Philippians 4:13 states, "I can do all things through Christ which strengtheneth me." Because we are Christians and have the very Spirit of Christ living inside of us, we should be able to accomplish whatever we set or determine in our minds to do. The strength and power of Christ resides on the inside of us. The Holy Spirit in us leads, guides, and directs us. John 14:26 says, "But the Comforter (Counselor, Helper, Intercessor, Advocate, Strengthener, Standby), the Holy Spirit, Whom the Father will send in My name [in My place, to represent Me and act on My behalf], He will teach you all things. And He will cause you to recall (will remind you of, bring to your remembrance) everything I have told you" (AMP).

We should be confident producers. God has made you in His image and likeness; He has equipped you with the Holy Spirit, and He has given you His Word. We should be ready, prepared, and operational. You can go forward confidently to use your sense to make dollars. He has given you everything you need to do this and to acquire your financial freedom. You must confidently move forward and use God's wisdom to be productive.

John 15:4–5 says this: "Dwell in me, and I will dwell in you. [Live in Me, and I will live in you.] Just as no branch can bear fruit of itself without abiding in (being vitally united to) the vine, neither can you bear fruit unless you abide in Me. I am the Vine; you are the branches. Whoever lives in Me and I in him bears much (abundant) fruit. However, apart from Me [cut off from vital union with Me] you can do nothing" (AMP). As children of God, Christians with Christ living on the inside of us through the Holy Spirit, we should be bearing much fruit and producing abundantly. Our streams should be flowing and bringing forth increase. Our witty ideas and innovation should be abundant. We should be producing much. Be confident—you have what you need. God has equipped you properly, appropriately, and abundantly.

As a matter of fact, God loves it when we produce in abundance. He loves it when we bear much fruit. John 15:8 says, "When you bear (produce) much fruit, My Father is honored and glorified, and you show and prove yourselves to be true followers of Mine" (AMP). God wants us to bear fruit and produce. He loves to bless us. He loves to be gracious to us. He wants us to do well in this earth. When we do, as His children, it brings glory to God and His name. It shows that as we follow Him and His Word, it brings good into our lives. When the nature of God was revealed to Moses, God proclaimed this in Exodus 34:5–6: "And the LORD descended in the cloud, and stood with him there, and proclaimed the name of the LORD. And the LORD passed by before him, and proclaimed, The LORD, The LORD God, merciful and gracious, longsuffering, and abundant in goodness and truth." It is God's nature to be gracious and abundant in goodness to us. He loves us, and He is waiting to be gracious to us. Even in Psalm 23:6, it says, "Surely goodness and mercy shall follow me all the days of my life: and I will dwell in the house of the LORD for ever." So go on this journey to financial freedom confidently, positively, and producing abundantly. God is with you. His Spirit is inside of you. His goodness and mercy is with you. And He wants to bless you abundantly.

Go forth to create, innovate, and pioneer in abundance. Know that your trust and confidence is in God. Know that you were created in His image and likeness. Use the sense (wisdom) God gave you to make dollars. As Christians, remember that since you are created in God's image and you have the mind of Christ, do not forget to use those dollars to do good works. Supply and give funding to support the kingdom of God here on earth so the gospel can be preached to every creature all over the world (Mark 16:15). Help take the gospel to all corners of the earth. We are blessed, and God makes sure that He honors His covenant and fulfills His promises to us. He also blesses us financially so that we can bless and do good to and for others.

There may be many obstacles on your road to financial freedom. No one is guaranteed a perfect, obstacle-free path when trying to accomplish or achieve his or her goals. Remember to take your journey one day at a time, one step at a time, and ask God to direct your path. It takes time to build anything. *Follow godly principles, and use your God-given wisdom.*

Review the chapters in this book often. Step out in faith, sow a seed, give it time to produce, and watch expectantly for your harvest. Be diligent in all your endeavors. Move forward progressively and confidently. Always know that God is with you. Seek Him and His Word for guidance and instruction continuously, for with God all things are possible. *Live a life of financial freedom!*

PRAYER FOR SALVATION AND PRAYER FOR BAPTISM WITH THE HOLY SPIRIT

IIIIIIIIIIIIIIIIIIIIIIIIIIIIIIIIIIIIIIIIII

Father, I come to You in the name of Jesus. Your Word states, "And it shall come to pass, that whosoever shall call on the name of the Lord shall be saved" (Acts 2:21). I am now coming to You and calling on You. I pray now and ask Jesus to come into my heart and be the Lord of my life, according to the scripture, Romans 10:9–10, which says, "That if thou shalt confess with thy mouth the

Lord Jesus, and shalt believe in thine heart that God hath raised him from the dead, thou shalt be saved. For with the heart man believeth unto righteousness; and with the mouth confession is made unto salvation." Lord, I pray that now. I confess with my mouth and believe in my heart that Jesus is the Lord of my life and that God raised Him from the dead. I am now a new person in Christ, a new creation. Old things have passed away, and I have been made new according to 2 Corinthians 5:17. I am now born again! I have been reborn; I am now a Christian. I am saved and a child of God Almighty!

Therefore, Father, I ask You to "fill" me with the Holy Spirit. I receive the Holy Spirit infilling now, and I expect to speak with other tongues as the Holy Spirit gives me utterance (Acts 2:4). Father, I thank You for the Holy Spirit. I thank You that I am a born again, Spirit-filled believer, and I put my trust in You and Your Word. I ask all of the above in Jesus' name. Amen!

ABOUT THE AUTHOR

||||||||||||||||||||||||||||||||||||

BISHOP ISAIAH S. Williams Jr., DD, was the pastor and founder of Jesus People Ministries, Inc., which includes Jesus People Ministries Church International, located in Miami, Florida. He was overseer of Right Connection Association until July 2, 2009, when he went to be with the Lord. Bishop Williams was also the president of ISWJR Ministries, founded as a ministry that infiltrates the world with the sincerity and simplicity of the gospel of Christ Jesus.

Bishop Williams was born and raised in the city of Miami, Florida, where he grew up as the great-grandson, grandson, and son of founding AME pastors and church stewards. It was at the age of twelve that he met his wife, Dr. Gloria, in secondary school, and they were married in June 1974. Bishop Williams has two daughters, Lori and Richelle.

Bishop Williams served in the United States Navy as a navy shipman. While in the military, before being called to the ministry, he was blessed to travel extensively throughout many different regions of the world. It was aboard the prestigious John F. Kennedy aircraft carrier that Isaiah Williams experienced a life-changing conversion that led to a personal relationship with Jesus Christ on February 26, 1977. By 1983, the call of God was confirmed and set in motion as Pastor Williams started the work of Jesus People Ministries (JPMCI). Since its beginning, the church has grown to over eight thousand members, and through its progressively growing membership, the ministry has an even larger number of partners throughout Florida, the United States, and the world. The heart of Jesus People Ministries Church is one of domestic and foreign missions outreach with an evangelistic thrust.

Isaiah Williams excelled as a student and athlete. He was awarded a basketball scholarship to John J. Pershing College (Beatrice, Nebraska), where he studied until he joined the United States Navy. He attended Miami Christian College, New Orleans Baptist Theological Seminary, and Dr. Lester Sumrall's World Harvest Bible College, where he received a diploma in biblical studies. In 1991, he received an honorary doctor of divinity degree from All Nations of Christ Institute International, a previous affiliate of Oral Roberts University. In 2004, he received an earned doctor of ministry degree from Vision International University in Ramona, California.

Isaiah Williams taught and proclaimed the truth

of the uncompromising Word of God with integrity, fervor, and sound character. He operated in the ministry office gifts of the apostle, prophet, pastor, and teacher, with the gifts of the Spirit in vivid manifestation. He was elevated to the office of bishop in 1996. He was an author and an acclaimed conference speaker. He was overseer of a vast number of affiliate ministers and ministries under the direction of ISWJR Ministries and Right Connection Ministries, Inc.

Bishop Williams was the founder of the Right Connection Association (RCA), an organization commissioned to assist pastors, leaders, and business professionals in understanding the tools required to lead a successful organization. He was also the president and CEO of the Justice, Potential, and Motivation (JPM) Centre, a center that serves as an oasis for economic and social development in the city of Miami Gardens and its neighboring sectors.

Bishop Williams was a spiritual voice to the community and a community activist. Under his leadership, JPMCI was presented a key to the city of Miami, Florida, the city of Opa-Locka, Florida, and the city of Rockledge, Florida. He also received numerous proclamations from cities throughout the South Florida area.

Bishop Williams was a devoted husband to his wife, Gloria, for thirty-five years, who is now the senior pastor and CEO of the ministry. Bishop Williams is honored every year at JPMCI's Founders Week event.

The first week of November is designated as a time to celebrate and honor this great man of God, a great person and a great leader.

CONTACT THE AUTHORS

||||||||||||||||||||||||||||||||||

We Want to Stay in Touch With You

Jesus People Ministries Church International (JPMCI) and Right Connection Ministries International (RCMI) would like to extend an invitation for you to stay in touch with us so that we can help you to grow and mature in the Word of God. We would like to help strengthen you in your daily walk as a Christian.

The JPMCI family of God extends our love to you, and we want to help you build a solid foundation in your walk with God. We are praying for you and would like to assure you that you are serving a great, powerful, and awesome God. He is filled with grace, mercy, goodness, and loving-kindness. Moreover, He desires to bestow them all on you.

Build your foundation on the chief cornerstone,

Jesus Christ. We are believing that God gives you the desires of your heart and that the dreams you are aspiring for will manifest in due season.

We want to hear from you! You can partner with us for kingdom business. Please contact us at the addresses below:

JESUS PEOPLE MINISTRIES CHURCH INTERNATIONAL
4055 N W 183RD STREET
MIAMI, FL 33055-2830

www.jesuspeoplemiami.org

RIGHT CONNECTION MINISTRIES INTERNATIONAL
P.O. BOX 172570
HIALEAH, FL 33017-2570

www.rightconnectionministries.org

OTHER BOOKS AND MATERIALS BY ISAIAH S. WILLIAMS JR., DD

||||||||||||||||||||||||||||||||||

Financial Freedom Workbook—Resource Manual/ Binder (FFWB-BD)

A guide full of information, exercises, and principles that will help you to be successful in your journey toward achieving financial freedom.

Financial Freedom Seminar CD Series—Resource CD Series (FFS-S6)

A collection of six (6) resourceful CDs that will help to build your knowledge of godly principles and finances. A good listening tool to help build your confidence and start you on your way to obtaining financial freedom.

Challenge to Change—Paperback (CTC-BK)

This inspiring book on change will encourage readers to embrace change. Change is good and necessary for growth and maturity. Get motivated to make the changes necessary for a successful, loyal, and devoted life to God.

Family Affairs: The Complete Work—CD Series (FAFTCW-S7)

A successful family connected to God. A collection of seven (7) signature CDs that teach the family about total allegiance to God. The complete work covers a range of family relationships, from business to marriage. Learn how to walk in the Word and follow the customs and methods needed for a successful family life. Move to new heights in your commitment as a family to serve God and honor His Word.

Other Exciting, Encouraging, and Life-Changing CD Series by Bishop Williams:

God Wants You to Prosper—CD Series (GWTP-S6)

Power Connection—CD Series (PCN-S3)

Hold Fast to Your Confidence—CD Series (HFTC-S3)

The Power of Favor—CD Series (TPF-S3)

Knowing Who Your Source Is—CD Series (KWSI-S2)

Increase On My Mind—CD Series (IOM-S2)